The Republic of Austin *tells us exactly where to feel the vibrations that link the present with the energy in the swelling lexicon of local lore. Ray Spivey's illustrations compliment the book beautifull*

author of *Not Between Brow...*

For those of us who love Austin, Texas, and its history, this collection of stories, written with the intent to bring history alive and to locate the sites where people made early Austin come into being, is a fine contribution to the understanding of our past.

— FRANK COOKSEY
Former Mayor of Austin

The Republic of Austin *vividly brings to life the early events that tested the young city's mettle and showed its knack for survival. Jeff Kerr's choice stories entertain and enlighten in equal measures.*

— SCOTT ZESCH
author of *The Captured: A True Story of Abduction by Indians on the Texas Frontier,*
winner of the TCU Texas Book Award

It's hard to put down this well-written collection of tales from Texas's past. Dr. Kerr weaves a rich tapestry of Central Texas stories and brings to life places we are already familiar with but don't really know. You can almost hear the hoofbeats down Congress Avenue as Dr. Kerr provides a new way of understanding our special city, like learning more about an old friend.

— LLOYD DOGGETT
U.S. Congressman, 25th District of Texas

Jeff Kerr's **The Republic of Austin** *is a page-turner in making the rich stories of our town and its people come alive. Full of murder, mystery, mayhem, the pioneer spirit, and love eternal, it's a great read and a good lesson for generations.*

— LUCI BAINES JOHNSON

Republic of Austin

Numbers on the map correspond to those in the "Visit the Sites" section at the end of each chapter.

THE REPUBLIC OF AUSTIN

BY

JEFFREY S. KERR

WITH ILLUSTRATIONS BY

RAY SPIVEY

AND

PHOTOGRAPHS BY
JEFFREY S. KERR

WATERLOO PRESS
AUSTIN, TEXAS

Waterloo Press
Austin History Center Association, Inc.
PO Box 2287
Austin, Texas 78768-2287

Cataloging-in-Publication Data

p.   cm.   illus.

1. Austin, Texas—History 2. Republic of Texas 3. Texas—History
4. United States of America—History, the West

F 394 A943 K68 2010   976.431 KE

ISBN 978-0-615-39035-2

Printed in the United States of America
by Morgan Printing in Austin, Texas

ACKNOWLEDGMENTS

I would like to thank the following people and organizations for their assistance in the creation of

THE REPUBLIC OF AUSTIN:

Ray Spivey, for generously agreeing to so beautifully illustrate each chapter,

Ricardo Puente, for the excellent maps,

Kathleen Davis Niendorff, for her editorial assistance and encouragement,

Waterloo Press and the Austin History Center Association, for believing in this project, and

Sharon, my wife, for her encouragement and support.

TABLE OF CONTENTS

Table of Contents

INTRODUCTION

"HISTORY IS BORING." What frustrated school child, tasked with memorizing a list of unfamiliar names and random dates, hasn't uttered these words? Such work is tedious, all the more so because it seems irrelevant, so unconnected to the student's life. Because the march of time has hidden or obliterated most physical links to the past, the student eventually puts down his or her work, walks outside, and enters an environment that might as well be on another planet, given how unrelated it seems to the images in most history books. The bored school child becomes a bored adult, one for whom the past is forgotten or, even worse, remembered inaccurately.

This is an unfortunate outcome. Not only because forgetting the past negatively impacts our present, but because ignoring the past, *our* past, means ignoring so many fascinating tales of courage, adventure, comedy, and tragedy. History is *NOT* boring. History is the collective sea of human experience from which we sprang and to which we will return. We are but temporarily washed up on the shore that is our present life; meanwhile, the currents of the past influence and, if we allow it, inform and entertain us.

Less than a mile from my suburban Austin home a 14-year-old girl died and was scalped by her Comanche kidnapper. For almost 20 years I passed this site in ignorance of the horrific deed which had been committed there. I can look out the window of my medical office near East 51st Street at the place where Indians left a man for dead after shooting and scalping him. The man survived. Modern Austin residents routinely refer to a creek bearing the man's name without realizing why they do so. An innkeeper's public beating of a Frenchman at Congress Avenue and 6th (Pecan) Street resulted in a diplomatic breach between France and the Republic of Texas, a fact known to few who pass the site today. Are these tidbits boring? Or do they spark a desire to know more?

The stories in this book are true. They involve real people engaged in life in and around Austin in its earliest days. Nevertheless, the stories inevitably contain inaccuracies. Most are based on personal recollections, some written down years after the fact. Where multiple accounts exist, discrepancies abound. So, if you were to ask whether Mirabeau Lamar *really* stood on top of a hill by the Colorado River and said, "This should be the seat of empire," I would answer, "I don't know, but that's what some people thought at the time."

Another caveat must be that the tales involving Indians are necessarily slanted toward the Anglo perspective. Because the Comanche, Lipan Apache, and other Austin-area Indians kept no written records, I have been unable to locate any first-hand native accounts of the events presented in this book. Nineteenth-century Anglo-Texans almost uniformly saw Indians as unworthy savages. As settler Jane Cazneau wrote, "as for the Indians, in his [the Anglo's] eyes they were only made to be killed."[1] This pervasive Anglo attitude influenced not only the individual's actions but official government policy. The Republic of Texas initiated a sweeping policy of ethnic cleansing that continued with statehood and resulted in the death or expulsion of most Texas Indians, "friendly" or not.[2] What rationale would the killer of the 14-year-old girl mentioned above have offered? I don't know. But he and his family had very likely suffered at the hands of the Anglos by the time of his deed. And, because of our Anglo predecessors, his modern descendants live a life much different and possibly poorer than the one he dreamed of for them.

I present the stories in *The Republic of Austin* as proof that history is anything *but* boring. Ray Spivey's original paintings offer a glimpse of how each site looked in the past, while the photographs, Ricardo Puente's maps, and map reference numbers at the end of each chapter provide a means of locating the places described in the story. Visit those sites today, stand on the exact spot of Sam Houston's presidential inauguration or Josiah Wilbarger's scalping, and discover that history is interesting, history is exciting, history is *alive!*

ENDNOTES

1. Marilyn McAdams Sibley, *Travelers in Texas 1761-1860* (Austin: University of Texas Press, 1967), p. 121.

2. For an excellent history of Anglo-Indian relations in Texas see Gary Anderson Clayton, *The Conquest of Texas: Ethnic Cleansing in the Promised Land, 1820-1875* (Norman: University of Oklahoma Press, 2005).

1

SCALPINGS, GHOSTS, AND DREAMS

IF THE BULLET THAT CREASED his spine had not temporarily paralyzed Josiah Wilbarger, his story would long ago have faded into oblivion. After all, violent clashes between Indians and Anglo colonists occurred with regularity on the Texas frontier. A wounded Wilbarger capable of movement would have flinched while being scalped. How easy, then, for his assailant to slice through his throat once the trophy had been secured? Mourning relatives would have buried the dead man; modern descendants might know his name but little else. Death would have swallowed an undistinguished life, save for the unlikely course taken by a small piece of flying lead.

Shortly after their wedding, Josiah Wilbarger and Margaret Barker bade farewell to friends and family in Pike County, Missouri, and traveled to Texas, landing in Matagorda December 26, 1827. In the spring of 1830, Josiah accompanied Stephen F. Austin to help survey the empressario's colony on the upper Colorado River. While on this trip he befriended fellow surveyor Reuben Hornsby. He also procured a land grant from Austin situated at the mouth of what is now known as Wilbarger Creek. Wilbarger wasted no time in moving his wife and young child to his new homestead. Two years later Reuben Hornsby occupied a riverfront tract about a mile to the west.

Reuben Hornsby's farm soon became a popular stopping place for those interested in settling in the region. Generous and hospitable, Reuben and wife Sarah welcomed not only the news brought from the United States by their guests, but also the protection afforded by increased numbers of men to defend against Indian attack. So it was that two Missourians, Standifer and Haynie, as well as a man named Christian and his wife, came to reside with the Hornsby family. One August day in 1832 Josiah Wilbarger agreed to guide Standifer, Haynie, Christian, and another prospective immigrant called Strother on a tour of the countryside. The five mounted men left from the Hornsby place and headed northwest.

As Wilbarger and his companions began inspecting land in the vicinity of upper Walnut Creek, one of the men noticed a lone Indian observing them from a neighboring ridge. Wilbarger signaled for the man to approach, but was ignored. When he began riding toward the man, the Indian pointed toward smoke drifting upward from a cluster of cedar at the base of the hill before urging his horse to flight. Wilbarger's party gave chase but lost their quarry near the head of Walnut Creek. Spooked by the rider's actions, as well as by the campfire's suggestion of other Indians in the area, the men determined to ride back to the safety of Hornsby's farm.

Noon found Wilbarger and his companions near a spring still several miles from home. Josiah urged the men to keep riding but the others, perhaps influenced by the blazing August sun, insisted upon stopping for lunch. Despite his concern, Wilbarger unsaddled and hobbled his horse. Christian and Strother followed suit. Showing more caution, Standifer and Haynie staked their horses to graze but left their saddles in place.

Rifle fire cracked suddenly from the brush. Strother fell mortally wounded; his companions dashed for cover. A brief firefight ensued, during which Christian received a ball in the thigh, shattering the bone. Wilbarger rushed over and propped Christian upright against a tree, but at the cost of a minor hip wound and an arrow through one calf. A bullet had smashed Christian's powder horn. Wilbarger checked the crippled man's rifle and found it loaded but not primed. He primed the weapon, returned it to Christian and, while diving again for his original cover, took an arrow through his other leg.

Seeing Strother dying and Christian hopelessly crippled, Standifer and Haynie each sprang for his horse. An unnerved Wilbarger pleaded for one of them to allow him to mount from behind. As he stumbled toward the riders a rifle ball pierced the back of his neck and exited through the chin. He fell, paralyzed but conscious. Standifer and Haynie escaped.

Indians rushed up to the downed men and quickly dispatched Christian and Strother by slitting their throats. Whoever approached Wilbarger saw a motionless man with an arrow protruding from each leg, a bleeding hip wound, and a gaping hole over the cervical spine. Deeming a throat cutting superfluous, the Indian instead stripped Wilbarger, grabbed his hair, and sliced at his scalp. Amazingly, Wilbarger felt no pain. As the skin was being ripped from his skull he experienced only a sound like distant thunder. Then he mercifully passed out.

Hours later Wilbarger awoke desperately thirsty. He dragged his bleeding body to a chilly pool of water, in which he lay for an hour. Sleep claimed him after the struggle back onto dry land. Thirsty again upon awakening, he returned to the pool, drank, and began crawling through the prairie towards Reuben Hornsby's house six miles away. Already maggots feasted in his wounds. This fearful realization provided strength enough to stand, and he stumbled to the southeast for about a quarter mile before collapsing under a large post oak tree.

Naked, sunburned, oozing blood, and wracked with pain, Josiah Wilbarger lay under the oak throughout a tortured night. But he was not alone. Owls hooted overhead, coyotes and wolves yipped and snarled in the distance, and suddenly there stood his sister Margaret Clifton who, unknown to Josiah at the time, had died the day before in Florissant, Missouri. "Brother Josiah," she told him, "you are too weak to go by yourself. Remain here, and friends will come to take care of you before the setting of the sun."

"Margaret, my sister, Margaret!" called the dying man. "Stay with me till they come!" But Margaret only turned to face the way home before fading into the darkness.

Sarah Hornsby undoubtedly fell asleep that night only with difficulty. She had heard the unequivocal report from Standifer and Haynie: Christian, Strother, and Wilbarger, dead; 50 Indians swarming over the bodies as the more fortunate men made their escape; the ghastly sight of one Indian yanking the scalp from Josiah Wilbarger's lifeless corpse. No one wanted to believe it, but this was not the first time Sarah Hornsby and the others of her household had heard such a tale. Death and life danced inextricably among them. Sarah Hornsby knew this and went to bed certain that a search party on the morrow would return with the bodies of her friends.

Yet during the night, while Josiah Wilbarger lay in tortured agony under the post oak tree, Sarah Hornsby learned otherwise. Shaking her husband Reuben awake, she excitedly reported that she had seen Wilbarger in a dream. Not his corpse, but a living, breathing man. Brushing aside his wife's unrealistic vision, Reuben urged her back to sleep.

Sarah woke again. This time she insisted to Reuben that she *had* seen Josiah and that he *lived*. He was naked, scalped, and otherwise wounded but, she exclaimed, "I *know* that Wilbarger is not dead."

No one would sleep any longer that night in the Hornsby house; Sarah would not allow it. After rousting the men from their beds she fed them breakfast and sped them on their way. Joseph Rogers, Reuben Hornsby, John Walters, and several others rode northward disbelieving that they would find any survivors. When Rogers, who rode in the lead, caught the first glimpse of the bloodied Wilbarger under his tree he shouted, "Here they are, boys" and steeled himself for the Indian fight he saw coming. But Josiah, hearing his rescuers approach, struggled to his feet and gasped, "Don't shoot, it is Wilbarger!"

Hornsby's burial mission now became a race to save Josiah Wilbarger's life. He and the others covered Strother and Christian with sheets and left them for later. They wrapped Wilbarger, naked except for a piece of sock that he had salvaged and used to cover his exposed skull, and placed him on a horse in front of Hornsby, the smallest of the rescuers. Back at the farm a vindicated Sarah Hornsby assumed nursing duties. Bear grease served as a healing salve for Wilbarger's wounds. Reuben's son Billy and Josiah's father-in-law Leman Barker constructed a sled, which was used a few days later to convey the recovering man back to his own house a mile downriver.

Josiah Wilbarger lived 11 years beyond having been shot, scalped, and left for dead. His unusual experiences turned him into a local celebrity. Visitors to the region seeking to meet him reported a congenial man who, in the tradition of the frontier, had carried on with his life as if nothing had happened. Ultimately, though, his head wound proved fatal. Scar tissue covered much of the exposed skull, but a small central spot remained bare, over which Wilbarger wore a small cap. The bone deteriorated anyway. In 1844 he accidentally struck his head on a low door frame. He became delirious and died several weeks later.

In 1836, three years after Wilbargar's scalping, Indians attacked the Hibbins family near its home in DeWitt's colony on the Colorado River. They took Sarah Hibbins and her two children while killing her mother and husband. Days later Sarah escaped from her kidnappers somewhere along what is now called Shoal Creek. She eluded them by wading through the creek all the way to its confluence with the Colorado, where she sought refuge in the home of Jacob Harrell. By chance Colonel Tumlinson and a company of rangers arrived shortly thereafter. After hearing of the plight of Sarah's child (one, an infant, had already been killed) they immediately pursued the Indians and overtook them the next morning. Their initial barrage killed two of the kidnappers; the rest scattered and fled, leaving the Hibbins child behind. As the rangers rummaged through the captured gear of the Indians, one of them picked up a rifle with a broken stock. He later returned it to its original owner, Josiah Wilbarger.

Josiah Wilbarger's travails and eventual martyrdom contributed significantly to the self-righteous mythology that early Anglo–Texans constructed about themselves. His brother, J. W. Wilbarger, author of the popular book *Indian Depredations in Texas,* stated that "this was the first blood shed in Travis county at the hands of the implacable savages. It was but the beginning, however, of a bloody era which was soon to dawn upon the people of the Colorado. . . today we enjoy the blessings of a prosperity, purchased with the blood and heroism of a sturdy class of pioneers whom any nation would delight to honor. There are but few of them left, but they stand like the giant oaks of the forest, storm beaten but living evidences of the distant past." Reading this today, one wonders to whom the Indians of 19th century Texas would have attributed the dawn of a "bloody era."

VISIT THE SITES

- Wilbarger and his companions were scouting the area at the head of Walnut Creek when they saw the lone Indian observing them. Walnut Creek originates near the intersection of Dorsett Road and Wycliff Lane in northwest Austin. The Indian was last seen on the southwest corner of the modern intersection of Braker Lane and MoPac Expressway. ⑤

- The attack on the Wilbarger party occurred about a half mile up Tannehill Branch Creek from Pecan Springs. The spring, now dry, is behind an apartment complex at 5020 Manor Road. This would place the fight about where the creek crosses 51st Street as it exits Bartholomew District Park. ⑥

- The post oak tree under which Hornsby and the others found Wilbarger stood at what is now the intersection of 51st Street and Old Manor Road. The historical marker that once marked the spot has been moved to Bartholomew District Park at the intersection of Berkman Drive and 51st Street. ⑦

- Josiah and Margaret Wilbarger are interred in the Texas State Cemetery at 909 Navasota Street in Austin. ⑧

ENDNOTES

1. The details of Josiah Wilbarger's story are from J. W. Wilbarger, *Indian Depredations in Texas* (Austin: Eakin Press, 1985, reprint of the original published by Hutchings Printing House in 1889), pp. 7-14, and John Henry Brown, *Indian Wars and Pioneers of Texas* (Austin: L. E. Daniell, 1880), pp. 23-25. J. W. Wilbarger was Josiah Wilbarger's brother while Brown had known Wilbarger as a young child in Pike County, Missouri, and as a young man in Austin in the early 1840's. Given J. W. Wilbarger's status as a family member of Josiah's, I estimate his to be the more accurate account.

2. J. W. Wilbarger states that the Indian escaped "about where James Rogers afterwards settled." Rogers' house stood near the modern intersection of Braker Lane and MoPac Expressway. Wilbarger, p. 9.

3. This spring is now known as Pecan Springs. It lies in Tannehill Branch Creek near 51st Street and Manor Road and flows only rarely.

4. For a more detailed account of the Hibbins attack, see Wilbarger, pp. 220-222.

5. Wilbarger, pp. 13-14.

Northeast view at the intersection of MoPac Expressway and Braker Lane, where Josiah Wilbarger and his companions saw the lone Indian waving at them in 1832.

View east along 51st Street at its intersection with Old Manor Road, one-time site of the post oak tree that the severely injured Josiah Wilbarger was found leaning against.

Historical marker commemorating Josiah Wilbarger in Bartholomew Park at East 51st Street and Berkman Drive. The small plaque at the base is for Wilbarger's companions Strother and Christian, both killed in the same attack in which Wilbarger was injured.

Josiah Wilbarger's grave in the Texas State Cemetery.

2

HORNSBY'S BEND

STEPHEN F. AUSTIN NEEDED SETTLERS and Reuben Hornsby needed land. With permission from the Mexican government, Austin had begun doling out land to American immigrants in 1823. By the time of Hornsby's 1830 arrival in Texas, American expatriates had already populated much of "Austin's Colony" along the Brazos and Colorado rivers. The native Georgian therefore had little choice but to head for the edge of Anglo settlement to claim his headright. He accepted a surveying job with Austin which took him far up the Colorado River, where he marked out a large swath[1] of rich prairie at a sharp bend in the river about 30 miles above Bastrop. He returned with his family in July 1832 to occupy what soon became known as Hornsby's Bend.

Hornsby had chosen his land well. One neighbor observed years later that "[a] more beautiful tract of land, even now, can nowhere be found than the league of land granted to Reuben Hornsby." Reuben quickly set to work developing his property. His wife Sarah tended to the task of raising their large brood of children. An unknown number of slaves also contributed their labor.

With Austin's founding as the seat of government in 1839, Hornsby's Bend became a popular rest stop along the road from Bastrop. The Hornsbys welcomed the company. Noah Smithwick recalled that "[they] opened their doors to all who chose to avail themselves of their hospitality. Thither in times of peril other families repaired for safety, and, if they needed it, more substantial aid was generously given."[2] J. W. Wilbarger, whose family farmed another bend in the Colorado between the Hornsbys and Bastrop, wrote, "Hornsby's house was always noted for hospitality, and he, like his neighbor Wilbarger [J. W.'s brother Josiah], was remarkable for those virtues and that personal courage which made them both marked men among the early settlers. Young men who from time to time came up to the frontier to look at the country made Hornsby's house a stopping place, and were always gladly welcomed . . . ."[3] Reuben's generosity extended beyond a meal and place to sleep, as noted by contemporary John Holland Jenkins, who claimed, "Reuben Hornsby, in moving back to his home after the Runaway Scrape,[4] had thoughtfully taken a supply of ammunition and it became generally known; the neighbors would frequently go to him for ammunition."[5] Because ammunition ranked among the more important of staples on the frontier, the Hornsby's largesse earned them no small measure of gratitude.

Many of the most memorable tales of frontier life along the upper Colorado River involve the Hornsbys and their land. Both Sarah and Reuben played prominent roles in the 1833 rescue of Josiah Wilbarger, scalped by Indians and left for dead.[6] Ten years later, son Joseph's daring helped save the life of Captain Coleman after he was captured and his traveling companion William Bell killed.[7] Reuben himself escaped death in the fall of 1837 when Indians attacked three men crossing his land on their way to Bastrop. Two of the men got away, but Joseph Rogers, who was riding a substandard mount, did not. After killing Rogers, the Indians headed toward the Hornsby's house. Working alone in a distant field but within sight of the house, Reuben would have been easy prey but for the quick action of one of his sons who spotted the Indians approaching and raced to his father with a fast horse.[8]

Shortly after returning home from the Runaway Scrape in May 1836, the Hornsbys participated in a larger, bloodier Indian encounter.[9] Three soldiers named Haggett, Williams, and Cain, who had assisted the family in its eastward retreat, stayed to help tend crops. About 10 o'clock one morning Haggett and Williams were hoeing one part of a corn field while Cain and the Hornsby sons worked in another when 10 to 15 Indians approached the former group bearing a white flag. The Indians encircled the pair before killing one man with a lance. The survivor burst through the circle, only to be felled by a rifle shot.

Meanwhile, Joe, Reuben Jr., and Malcolm Hornsby and the soldier Cain ascended the river bank just as Williams and Haggett died. Billy Hornsby had remained at his plow while his companions went for water; with his back to the attackers he had no hint of danger. But shouts from the returning laborers alerted Billy, who left his plow and team in the field and sprinted toward the river.

Reuben Sr., Sarah, and 5-year-old Thomas Hornsby were back at the house with a woman named Castner. Several times Thomas wandered out to the porch to play, only to immediately return with a warning of Indians in the distance. The adults dismissed the warnings as a childish game until Reuben, tired of the constant interruptions, went outside to see for himself. Seeing the Indians approach Williams and Haggett, Hornsby grabbed three rifles and started toward them but quickly realized that the two men were beyond assistance. He returned to the house and instructed the two women to don men's clothing. After telling Thomas to stay inside, the three adults paraded about the yard in a show of force, which must have worked, for the Indians did not attack. They did, however, make off with a large number of livestock.

Unarmed and helpless, Cain and the four Hornsby brothers swam across the river and fled the area. They later crossed back over the river and made their way to within a mile of home, where they stopped and waited for darkness. Having seen the initial attack only from a great distance, they had mistaken the killers for Mexican soldiers rather than Indians and feared that an even larger Mexican force might still be lingering nearby. Hunger eventually enticed them back to the Hornsby house, where Billy and Malcolm agreed to investigate further. A noise alerted Sarah Hornsby to their presence, who called to her husband that the Indians had returned. Recognizing her voice, Billy and Malcolm revealed themselves and called for the others to join them. As J. W. Wilbarger observed, "[t]he joyful meeting can better be imagined than described, for up to this time neither party knew what had been the fate of the other."[10]

The abundance of game at Hornsby's Bend played a pivotal role in another encounter later that same year. John Holland Jenkins recalled that Hornsby's land provided the best bear hunting in the region.[11] But it was the prospect of hunting wild cattle that drew three men, Harris, Blakey, and an unnamed third, up from nearby Webber's Prairie. After spending the night at the Hornsby house, the trio of hunters crossed the river and began their search.[12] As Harris and the anonymous man climbed out of a shallow ravine, several Indians fired rifles at the men, killing them instantly. Blakey trailed just enough to enable him to wheel his horse and escape. A later search party found the dead men's scalped, dismembered and disemboweled torsos. A short distance away were the remains of a fire, where the Indians had ritually cooked and eaten the men's hearts and parts of their limbs.[13]

With the founding and construction of Austin in 1839, traffic boomed along the road from Bastrop leading past Hornsby's Bend. Crews set to work felling trees in the pine forest surrounding Bastrop. Other men found economic opportunity in hauling the raw lumber and sawed planks to Austin. One such man was Hamilton White who, after securing a contract with government agent Edwin Waller, ordered one of his slaves to do the actual hauling.

White's man started from Bastrop one day not only with a load of lumber, but with $300 of White's money that he was to deliver to an Austin creditor. On the second day of the journey he stopped at Hornsby's Bend for the night. Late the next morning, when Sarah Hornsby asked the man why he had not yet moved on, he replied that he feared the possibility of Indian attack while traveling alone through unsettled country. Sarah told him he could stay and wait for another traveler to come by. But the slave recalled his instructions from White not to delay, so with great reluctance finally set out alone. Some time later travelers John Wilbarger and a companion saw what they at first took for a man sleeping in the bushes at Walnut Creek. Closer inspection revealed the scalped and lifeless body of Hamilton White's slave. The absence of the $300 led many to speculate that white thieves, rather than Indians, had killed the man.[14]

Finally, in June 1845 Reuben and Sarah Hornsby lost their son Daniel as a result of mistaken identity. An unnamed Comanche had been shot by Captain Coleman in a fight on the Pedernales River. Some time later the man saw Daniel Hornsby at a trading post and, mistaking him for Coleman, vowed revenge. Hearing of the threat, an Indian agent named Sloat sought out the Comanche to warn him off. The man shrugged off the warning and boasted that, not only could no white man harm him, but he had been the one to kill 14-year-old Emma Simpson near Austin the previous year.[15]

If Daniel Hornsby knew of this threat to his life, it didn't stop him from going fishing near the Hornsby homestead with his friend William Adkisson. As the two men fished from the bank, the vengeful Comanche and several companions speared them from behind. Several arrows pierced Hornsby as he tumbled into the water. The wounded Adkisson successfully swam across the river before dying on the opposite bank. When found, the dead man bore multiple stab wounds in his side, as if one of the attackers had swum alongside him while jabbing him repeatedly with a knife or arrow.

When the two young men failed to return to the Hornsby house that evening, several men set out to find them. They came across Adkisson's scalped corpse at the scene of his death, whereas Daniel Hornsby had floated about a mile and a half downstream. Some distance upstream searchers encountered a drawing in the sand of two coffins, each with an arrow stuck in it. The killers escaped. Anson Jones observed later that the deaths were "the result of a personal hatred and vow of revenge on the part of a Comanche Indian."[16]

Despite the violence of the 1830s and '40s, Reuben, Sarah, and the rest of the Hornsby clan not only held on, but prospered at Hornsby's Bend. Sarah died in 1862. Reuben lasted another 17 years, finally succumbing in 1879 at the age of 86. Although the house he built is long gone, the Hornsby name lives on as an appellation for numerous schools, churches, and landscape features throughout southeastern Travis County.

VISIT THE SITES

- Hornsby Cemetery is along FM 969 (Webberville Road) about 3.5 miles east of U. S. Highway 183 (Ed Bluestein Boulevard). A small sign on the south side of the road marks the turnoff. The historical marker for the Hornsbys' house is on the right about 0.2 miles beyond the turn. The cemetery is at the end of the road. Reuben, Sarah, and many other members of the Hornsby clan are buried there. There is a memorial for Daniel Hornsby and William Adkisson just beyond the wall at the cemetery's far end. Of note, the burial ground also contains the grave of Reuben's and Sarah's great-grandson, baseball Hall-of-Famer Rogers Hornsby. ②

- There is a historical marker nearby for Hornsby's Bend on the south side of FM 969 between the crossings for FM 973 and Texas Highway 130. ③

- Hamilton White's slave died about where FM 969 crosses Walnut Creek. The closest street intersection is that with Johnny Morris Road just east of the crossing. ④

ENDNOTES

1. At the time a married settler's headright consisted of "a league and labor" of land. The larger league, at 4428 acres, provided grazing for cattle while the 177-acre labor served for growing crops. *Handbook of Texas Online,* s.v. "Land Grants," http://www.tshaonline.org/handbook/online/articles/LL/mpl1.html (accessed March 20, 2010).

2. Noah Smithwick, *The Evolution of a State or Recollections of Old Texas Days* (Austin: University of Texas Press, 1984), p. 192.

3. J.W. Wilbarger, *Indian Depredations in Texas* (Austin: Eakin Press, 1985, reprint of the original published by the author in 1889), p. 8.

4. During the Texas Revolution, many Anglo settlers fled eastward in early 1836 to escape the threat of the advancing Mexican army. This became known as the Runaway Scrape. *Handbook of Texas Online,* s.v. "Runaway Scrape," http://www.tshaonline.org/handbook/online/articles/RR/pfr1.html (accessed March 22, 2010).

5. John Holmes Jenkins, III, ed., *Recollections of Early Texas: The Memoirs of John Holland Jenkins* (Austin: University of Texas Press, 2003), pp. 46.

6. See the chapter "Scalpings, Ghosts, and Dreams."

7. See the chapter "Captain Coleman's Lucky Break."

8. Wilbarger, pp. 261-262.

9. Details are from Wilbarger, pp. 255-259, and Jenkins, pp. 45-46.

10. Wilbarger, p. 259.

11. Jenkins, p. 234.

12. This would have placed them about where Austin Bergstrom International Airport now stands.

13. Wilbarger, p. 259.

14. Wilbarger, pp. 266-267, and Mary Starr Barkley, *History of Travis County and Austin 1839-1899* (Austin: Austin Printing Company, 1981), p. 35.

15. See the chapter "A Young Girl's Death."

16. Anson Jones, *Memoranda and Official Correspondence Relating to the Republic of Texas, its History and Annexation* (Chicago: The Rio Grande Press, Inc., 1966), p 473.

Historical marker for the site of Reuben and Sarah Hornsby's house at Hornsby's Bend. The Hornsby family cemetery lies at the end of the pictured road.

Within the Hornsby family cemetery are the graves of Reuben and Sarah Hornsby and many of their descendants. Reuben and Sarah are beneath the small obelisk against the stone wall at center right. Their more famous great-grandson Rogers Hornsby, a member of the Baseball Hall of Fame, lies nearby.

Left: Grave of Joseph Hornsby. Despite the marker's inscription, Hornsby and his companion James Edmondson were able to save only Alexander Coleman; William Bell died at the hands of the attacking Indians (see the chapter "Captain Coleman's Lucky Break").

TO
JOSEPHUS HORNSBY
MAR. 15, 1822
OCT. 21, 1862
SON OF REUBEN HORNSBY; SETTLED
HERE, 1832; BASTROP RANGER, 1837
IN FLORES FIGHT, 1839
BATTLE OF PLUM CREEK, 1840
BRUSHY FIGHT, 1840; VASQUEZ AND
WOLL CAMPAIGNS, 1842; LED FIGHT
AGAINST INDIANS FROM WHOM
HE RESCUED WILLIAM BELL AND
ALEXANDER COLEMAN IN AUSTIN, 1842
HIS WIFE
ELIZA ANN LANE
FEB. 14, 1830
SEPT. 6, 1892

Erected by the State of Texas
1936

Right: This marker in the Hornsby family cemetery commemorates four of the Anglo settlers killed by Indians at Hornsby's Bend, including Daniel Hornsby, son of Reuben and Sarah.

TO
JOHN WILLIAMS
AND
HOWELL HAGGETT
KILLED BY INDIANS IN MAY, 1836
WHILE DETAILED FROM
CAPTAIN JOHN J. TUMLINSON'S
COMPANY OF RANGERS
TO HELP PROTECT THE FAMILIES
OF THE HORNSBY'S SETTLEMENT
ON RETURNING FROM THE
"RUN AWAY SCRAPE"
TO
WILLIAM ATKINSON
PIONEER RANGER
BURIED NEAR
DANIEL HORNSBY
THEY BOTH WERE KILLED BY INDIANS
JUNE 7, 1840

Erected by the State of Texas
1936

Top: This is the oldest section of the Hornsby family cemetery, in which Reuben, Sarah, and several of their sons are buried.

Bottom: Historical marker on FM 969 indicating the site of Reuben Hornsby's original land grant on the upper Colorado River, which came to be known as Hornsby's Bend.

3

JACOB HARRELL MOVES WEST

IN THE FALL OF 1838, Republic of Texas Vice President Mirabeau Lamar toured the western frontier of the nation he hoped soon to lead. Searching for votes in the upcoming presidential election, Lamar also desired to see for himself the lush valley of the Colorado River. At Bastrop, the farthermost Anglo town on the Colorado, the Vice President picked up an escort of several Texas Rangers and headed upriver. A 30-mile ride brought the group to a broad plain stretched between a sharp bend in the river that was home to Reuben Hornsby, who with his family had occupied the land since 1832. Hornsby had already acquired a reputation as a gracious host; Lamar and his party undoubtedly stopped at Hornsby's Bend to rest and inquire about the region.

Reuben Hornsby would have told Vice President Lamar that his was no longer the last outpost on the Colorado River. In 1833 he had been joined at Hornsby's Bend by Jacob Harrell and his family. Two years later, Harrell moved into a tent farther upriver at a spot subsequently known as Waterloo. Once he had constructed sturdier accommodations, Harrell returned for his wife and children. The Harrell cabin now claimed the distinction as the uppermost Anglo settlement on the Colorado River.[1]

A ride of several hours beyond Hornsby's Bend brought Mirabeau Lamar to the base of a ravine near the mouth of modern-day Shoal Creek, where he encountered the cluster of cabins that was the unincorporated village of Waterloo. He received a warm welcome from Jacob Harrell, who offered to put up the Vice President and his party for a few days. The tale of Mirabeau Lamar's stay at Waterloo is reserved for another chapter[2], but suffice it to say that the presidential candidate gained a passionate appreciation for the region's potential.

Mirabeau Lamar easily won the 1838 presidential election. The new President dreamed of a vast Texan empire that would one day extend to the Pacific Ocean. The key to financing the dream was to divert Santa Fe's rich trade between Mexico and the United States toward Texas. The lure was to be a new and prosperous capital city on the banks of the upper Colorado. The planned metropolis would receive goods overland from Santa Fe, ship them downriver to Galveston, from which place ships would transport them to lucrative American markets and beyond. Substantial time, and therefore money, would be saved by using the waterway; those savings would guarantee the idea's success.

Lamar's stay at Jacob Harrell's cabin convinced him that Waterloo provided the perfect location for a new capital. He steered a site selection commission toward his preferred location and must have been pleased when the commissioners recommended it to Congress in April 1839. Although more practical considerations undoubtedly played a larger role in convincing commissioners of Waterloo's appeal, their report noted that "[t]he imagination of even the romantic will not be disappointed on viewing the Valley of the Colorado . . . ."[3]

Even before the commission announced its selection of Waterloo, it petitioned the Bastrop County court to condemn the acreage required for construction of the new seat of government. Standing in for Jacob Harrell at the March 23rd hearing, William Pinkney Hill accepted $3 an acre for Harrell's land.[4] In light of subsequent events it seems plausible that Harrell knew he would be able to remain in his home. Strictly speaking, however, he would have to bid on the property at the government auction that would parcel out city lots.

Lamar charged Edwin Waller with the enormous task of building a city from scratch. Immediately upon arriving at Waterloo in May 1839, the agent put his several hundred laborers to work. He laid out a square grid of streets stretching north from the river and situated roughly between Shoal and Waller creeks. And on August 1, 1839, he stood before a group of prospective buyers that included Jacob Harrell and began the task of auctioning off city land.

Jacob Harrell purchased four lots from the government that day, including the two on the west side of Congress Avenue at its intersection with Water (later renamed 1st and, later still, Cesar Chavez) Street.[5] At the auction's conclusion, Edwin Waller refunded the $150 down payment on Lot 2, which was being donated to Harrell by Congress. Lots facing Congress Avenue are numbered one through six, from south to north. Logic suggests that Lot 2 was the site of Jacob Harrell's cabin, the first building at Waterloo, and therefore the first in the city of Austin.

By the time of the first lot auction, Edwin Waller likely knew Jacob Harrell well. As a blacksmith, Harrell helped maintain the tools of Waller's labor force. He also erected a pen for butchering the animals used to feed the men. In 1847 Harrell served a term as Austin mayor. A year later he moved sixteen miles north to the Williamson County settlement of Brushy Creek. When postal officials asked the town to change its name, Harrell and neighbor Thomas Oatts suggested "Round Rock," after the shape of the large piece of limestone in Brushy Creek from which the men liked to fish. Harrell died of flux[6] August 23, 1853.

VISIT THE SITES

- At the first auction of city lots in 1839, Jacob Harrell purchased lots one and two on the west side of Congress Avenue between Cesar Chavez (Water) and 2nd (Live Oak) streets, which comprise the southernmost third of that city block. ❶

- The round rock fished on by Jacob Harrell and Thomas Oatts sits in Brushy Creek at its crossing with Chisholm Trail Road in the city of Round Rock. Park in the lot on the southwest corner of the intersection and walk across the street to see the rock. Don't miss the wagon wheel ruts from the old Chisholm Trail on the rocky north bank of the creek. ❾

ENDNOTES

1. *Handbook of Texas Online*, s.v. "Harrell, Jacob M.," http://www.tsha.utexas.edu/handbook/online/articles/HH/fha77.html (accessed November 5, 2008).

2. See the chapter "A Buffalo's Waterloo."

3. Ernest Wallace, David M. Vigness, and George B. Ward, *Documents of Texas History* (Austin: Texas State Historical Association, 2002), p. 132.

4. Seat of Government Papers, Texas State Archives.

5. One of these, Block 33 Lot 6, in the 400 block of East Cedar (4th), Harrell forfeited for nonpayment February 1, 1840. The other was Block 26 Lot 4 at the southeast corner of San Antonio and West Cypress (3rd) streets. Austin and Galveston City Lots, Texas State Archives.

6. The common term at the time for bloody diarrhea.

Jacob Harrell's cabin, the first building in Austin, most likely sat in what is now the footprint of the 100 Congress Building. Harrell purchased the leftmost third of this block in the city's first lot auction August 1, 1839.

Jacob Harrell's cabin sat on land directly behind the pickup truck seen in this photo looking west at Cesar Chavez (Water) Street and Congress Avenue.

Is Jacob Harrell's cabin depicted here? In this 1840 Edward Hall painting of Austin, Congress Avenue runs from the river into the distance. The painting is not to scale, but the cabin at lower left sits about where Harrell's two Congress Avenue lots were.

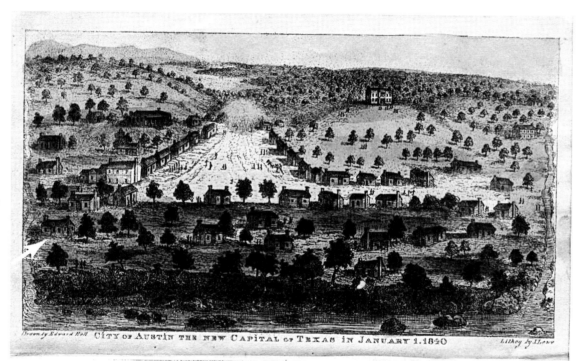

CITY OF AUSTIN THE NEW CAPITAL OF TEXAS IN JANUARY 1. 1840

The round rock of Round Rock, Texas, from which Jacob Harrell and Thomas Oatts enjoyed catching fish in Brushy Creek.

4

A BUFFALO'S WATERLOO

WHAT DID TEXAS VICE PRESIDENT Mirabeau Lamar see upon his arrival in the frontier town of Waterloo in the fall of 1838? Not much. Only a handful of cabins clustered on the north bank of the Colorado River not far from the best low water crossing in the area gave evidence to Lamar's concept of civilization. No streets yet existed to define a town. Founder Edward Burleson's plans called for streets, of course, but first he had to sell enough town lots to justify the expense. What Lamar saw, therefore, bore little resemblance to an actual municipality.[1]

Not that Lamar had expected anything different on his trip west. He knew that once he had traveled beyond Bastrop, 30 miles downriver from Waterloo, he had passed the last substantial Anglo settlement on the Colorado. The farms of Josiah Wilbarger and Reuben Hornsby prospered defiantly in the intervening wilderness, but little else broke the monotony of the seemingly endless prairie. At Walnut Creek, Lamar and his party had paused for the night at Fort Coleman. That once proud stockade now lay abandoned and in ruins, its walls and blockhouses mostly dismantled and hauled away for other building projects.[2]

Lamar's arrival substantially boosted Waterloo's tiny population. James Rice, Willis Avery, and four more Texas Rangers were along to protect the Vice President. Good friend Edward Fontaine and his slave Jacob came along as well.[3] The party found a willing host in Jacob Harrell, who had been the first of Waterloo's few residents to settle on the site when he moved his family up from Reuben Hornsby's place in 1835. At supper that first evening, Harrell likely heard Lamar speak of the upcoming presidential election and Lamar's excellent chances of winning it.

As the first popularly elected Vice President of the Republic of Texas, Mirabeau Lamar naturally possessed an edge in the presidential contest. His real advantage, though, stemmed from the recent deaths of his two main challengers. Today such events would spawn a mountain of conspiracy theories, but no one in 1838 blamed Lamar for Peter Grayson's suicide or a drunken James Collinsworth's accidental drowning in Galveston Bay.[4] Nevertheless, despite the near certainty of his victory, Lamar heeded the advice of friends and embarked on the western campaign swing that brought him to Waterloo.[5]

Mirabeau Lamar's true interest in the region of the upper Colorado River lay not with winning votes but with building empire. In those days a lucrative trade from the Mexican interior passed through Santa Fe on its way to St. Louis and American markets beyond. The arduous overland trip took months. Lamar envisioned diverting this trade to a Texas capital city on the Colorado River, from which goods could be floated downriver to the Gulf of Mexico, transferred to cargo ships, and sailed to the American east coast. The Vice President's rosy outlook also foresaw Santa Fe residents transferring allegiance from what he felt to be a decrepit Mexican government to the rising lone star of the Republic of Texas. And

Lamar saw no reason to stop with the acquisition of Santa Fe. To the west he saw only more Mexicans, deemed by him incapable of possessing the land, and Indians, deemed unworthy. To the Republic of Texas would fall the task of civilizing this vast wilderness, the successful completion of which would plant the Texas flag on the Pacific coast.[6]

Such was Mirabeau Lamar's state of mind as he breakfasted in the Waterloo cabin of Jacob Harrell when Harrell's young son burst into the room to report enormous numbers of buffalo in the vicinity. The men grabbed their weapons and left. Once mounted, they rode north up a muddy ravine that intersected the river. There they encountered the sight that so consistently thrilled early Anglo–Texans and that seems so unimaginable to us today: hundreds and thousands of buffalo scattered across the landscape to the horizon. Rather than employ the easier but less exciting method of picking off animals from afar with their rifles, Lamar and his companions charged among the beasts and blazed away with pistols. Later, the men realized that Lamar had felled by far the largest prey, a mammoth bull that dwarfed anything they had ever seen. The animal died at what months later became the intersection of Austin's Congress Avenue and Hickory (8th) Street.

Later the hunters gathered to a pre-arranged bugle call atop the hill at the head of the ravine. Looking south toward the river, all admired the beautiful scenery that stretched before them. But it was Mirabeau Lamar, a romantic dreamer who wrote poetry in his spare time, who carried his thoughts beyond the pleasure of the moment to proclaim, "This should be the seat of future empire!"[7]

VISIT THE SITES

- The historical marker for Fort Coleman may be seen on the south side of Martin Luther King Boulevard across from the turnoff for Russett Hill Road. ①

- Jacob Harrell's cabin site is the lower third of the west side of Congress Avenue between Cesar Chavez (Water) and 2nd (Live Oak) streets. ❶

- Mirabeau Lamar shot his buffalo at what is now the intersection of Congress Avenue and 8th (Hickory) Street. ❷

- Lamar's proclamation about empire was delivered from atop the hill on which the capitol now sits. In 1838 a grove of ancient live oak trees grew on the hill's summit. To achieve his sweeping view of the Colorado River, Lamar must therefore have been standing on the southern slope of this hill. The modern view from the steps of the capitol building remains magnificent. ❸

ENDNOTES

1. The Texas legislature did not approve Waterloo's incorporation until January 1839. The following April the town was condemned and purchased by the government for the construction of Austin. Seat of Government papers, Texas State Archives.

2. *Handbook of Texas Online*, s.v. "Fort Colorado" http://www.tsha.utexas.edu/handbook/online/articles/FF/qcf1.html (accessed May 28, 2006).

3. Jacob's presence is not certain. Mary Starr Barkley, *History of Travis County and Austin 1839-1899* (Austin: Austin Printing Company, 1981), p. 13.

4. Many, however, also saw Collinsworth's death a suicide. *Handbook of Texas Online*, s.v. "Collinsworth, James," http://www.tsha.utexas.edu/handbook/online/articles/CC/fco97.html (accessed May 28, 2006).

5. Supporter James Webb wrote Lamar, "It is the opinion of several of your friends with whom I have conversed, that a trip up the Country would be serviceable to you. I think so too." Charles Adams Gulick, Jr., ed., *The Papers of Mirabeau Buonaparte Lamar, vol. 2* (Austin: Texas State Library, 1922), p. 757.

6. Lamar offered a glimpse of his plans for westward expansion in his 1838 inaugural presidential address to Congress, in which he said, ". . . when I view her [Texas'] vast extent of territory, stretching from the Sabine to the Pacific and away to the South West as far as the obstinacy of the enemy may render it necessary for the sword to make the boundary . . . ." Gulick, Item number 913.

7. Alex W. Terrell, "The City of Austin From 1839 to 1865," (Volume 014, No. 2), *Southwestern Historical Quarterly Online*, pp. 113-128. http://www.tsha.utexas.edu/publicatons/journals/shq/online/v014/n2/article_2.html

Top: Looking west along 8th (Hickory) Street at its intersection with Congress Avenue. In 1838, before the city of Austin was built, Mirabeau Lamar shot an enormous buffalo at this location.

Bottom: Looking east along 8th (Hickory) Street at the same intersection. Notice that both views show a rise in the distance. Edwin Waller, who laid out Austin's streets in 1839, took advantage of the natural ravine running south to the Colorado River by using it for the town's major thoroughfare, Congress Avenue.

View south along Congress Avenue at 8th (Hickory) Street. Tall prairie grass dominated here in 1838. At what later became 4th (Cedar) Street a mixed forest took over. Among the trees stood the cluster of cabins comprising the town of Waterloo.

5

DEATH ON WEBBER'S PRAIRIE[1]

COLONEL JOHN MOORE LIKELY GAVE little thought to the long-term consequences of his intended actions as he peered into the pre-dawn darkness. Before him lay a large village, erected by the Comanche on the upper San Saba River in 1839 as a safe place to wait for the buffalo hunts that warmer weather would bring. Moore's hundred-man force consisted of an even mix of fellow Anglos and Lipan Apache allies. At his signal, they attacked. Without knowing it, Moore had just sentenced Elizabeth Coleman and her son Albert to death.

Caught completely by surprise, the Comanche mounted a feeble defense. Members of the attacking force quickly overwhelmed the village, "killing indiscriminately a number of all ages and sexes."[2] Moore's victory resulted in an untold number of Comanche orphans, widows, and grief-stricken families.

Four days later Elizabeth Coleman fed her children breakfast before going outside to tend to her vegetable garden. Elizabeth had worked hard to feed her family since losing her husband Robert two years earlier in a Brazos River drowning accident. And with the help of oldest son Albert, now 15, she had succeeded. With Albert quickly approaching manhood, she undoubtedly anticipated an easing of her burden.

The Coleman home sat in the lush bottomland of the Colorado River at Webber's Prairie.[3] On the morning of February 18, 1839, a large number of revenge-minded Comanche burst from cover and sprinted toward Elizabeth and her children. Albert and two daughters, ages nine and 11, gained the relative safety of the cabin. Elizabeth made it to the doorway, but as she turned to look for 5-year-old Tommy an arrow sliced through her throat. Albert dragged her inside and bolted the door. An Indian scooped up Tommy as a prize of war.

For a while Albert held his own in a desperate battle for survival. Aiming through cracks in the walls, he fired his breech-loading rifle several times before a shot from one of the Indians shattered the stock. A subsequent shot killed him. His terrified sisters sought shelter under a bed while attackers poked lances at them through gaps in the wall. When the Indians left to investigate loud yelling in the distance, the girls fled the house to hide in nearby woods.

Anglo pursuit of the raiders culminated the next day in a running battle along Brushy Creek about ten miles to the north. When John Grumbles, leader of the first group to catch up to the Comanche, realized that his small force was no match for the 200-300 Indians arrayed against him, he wisely retreated and sent men to gather reinforcements. Jacob Burleson[4] and James Rogers responded with about 50 men. When Burleson ordered the men in his immediate vicinity to dismount and attack, only a few obeyed. The rest, spooked by the surprisingly large number of the enemy, began a retreat. A 14-year-old boy who had obeyed Burleson's order jumped on his horse to follow without untying the animal. Burleson dashed over and freed the boy's mount but in attempting to regain his own saddle was killed with a shot to the head.

Elizabeth Coleman's daughters were found by John Anderson[5], who took them to the house of George Davis for safekeeping. There was no rescuer, though, for young Tommy. The boy spent the rest of his childhood with the Comanche before being sold back to his people. According to John Holland Jenkins, a participant in the Brushy Creek fight, Tommie had "been so imbued with their [the Comanche] ideas and habits that he went back to them, never feeling satisfied among the whites."[6]

VISIT THE SITES

- There is an historical marker for the Coleman home on the south side of FM 969 between the towns of Webberville and Utley.
- The Battle of Brushy Creek is commemorated by a marker along State Highway 95 about four miles south of Taylor. Look for a sign pointing west along a dirt road just south of Old Coupland Road (County Road 452).

ENDNOTES

1. Details of this chapter are mostly from J.W. Wilbarger, *Indian Depredations in Texas* (Austin: Eakin Press, 1985, reprint of the original 1889 edition by Hutchings Printing House), pp. 144-150 and John Holland Jenkins, III, ed., *Recollections of Early Texas: The Memoirs of John Holland Jenkins* (Austin: University of Texas Press, 2003), pp. 56-60.

2. Wilbarger, p. 145.

3. Named for the region's first Anglo settler, John Webber, who received his headright in 1832. Webber married an emancipated slave, with whom he had 11 children. In 1853, under pressure from many of his slave-owning neighbors, he moved to the Rio Grande Valley. *Handbook of Texas Online*, s.v. "Webber, John Ferdinand," http://www.tshaonline.org/handbook/online/articles/WW/fwe59.html (accessed July 18, 2010).

4. Jacob was the brother of Edward Burleson, who also participated in the battle and was elected Vice President in 1841. Jenkins, p. 60.

5. Anderson, who participated in the Battle of San Jacinto at the age of 17, studied law with Barrie Gillespie at Webber's Prairie. President Sam Houston named him district attorney for the Fourth Judicial District in 1844, thereby making Anderson a member of the Supreme Court. Anderson died at age 30 in 1849. *Handbook of Texas Online*, s.v. "Anderson, John D.," http://www.tshaonline.org/handbook/online/articles/AA/fan7.html (accessed July 18, 2010).

6. Jenkins, p. 60.

SITE OF THE HOME OF
COL. ROBERT M. COLEMAN
(1799—1837)

SIGNER OF THE TEXAS
DECLARATION OF INDEPENDENCE
AIDE-DE-CAMP TO GEN. HOUSTON AT
SAN JACINTO
COMMANDER OF A REGIMENT OF RANGERS
1836

HERE HIS WIDOW
MRS. ELIZABETH COLEMAN
AND SON, ALBERT V. COLEMAN
WERE KILLED BY INDIANS
AND THOMAS COLEMAN, AGED FIVE,
WAS CAPTURED
FEBRUARY 18, 1839

*Historical marker
indicating the site of
the Coleman home on
FM 969 between
Austin and Bastrop.*

6

BIRTH OF A CITY

THE OLD MAN HAD SEEN ENOUGH change. Seventy-two years after his 1839 arrival in Austin, he shuffled along the streets and sidewalks of a city hardly recognizable as the one he had helped construct. He could remember when a stroll down Congress Avenue involved dodging tree stumps and livestock. He had experienced the throat-gripping fear of expected Indian attack during the trip north to haul timber back from what was now Monroe Shipe's new Hyde Park subdivision. He recalled the crude blockhouses made of that timber, buildings that had mostly rotted away or yielded to sturdier stone constructions by the day in 1911 when he sat down to compose his letter. Everything had changed from that earlier time, everything was different. He had endured long enough that nothing remained within the city's original square mile to remind him of his youth.

Except for the trees: live oaks, with their thick, twisted, ancient trunks and their spreading canopies still shading the ground below. Ground that had once been covered by knee-high grass while being trod upon by a younger version of himself, as well as by a host of other men and women instrumental in creating the city. Ground that now lay strewn with trash and rubble.

Ninety-year-old John Darlington wanted to save those trees. Not only because of their antiquity, but also because of the vital role they had played in the city's history. And with his letter to the editor of the *Austin Statesman,* Darlington hoped to stir others to take up his cause:

> The first sale of city lots was made by auction under some live oak trees on the north side of a public square. . . . They still stand there, and I write to suggest that some action should be taken by the city authorities to preserve these trees and protect them. When I am dead no one will remain who can identify the spot.[1]

On August 1, 1839, at the age of 18, John Darlington had pushed his way through the thick rye surrounding those live oak trees to join the throng gathered around government agent Edwin Waller and auctioneer J. T. Doswell. Entrusted by Republic of Texas President Mirabeau Lamar to supervise construction of the new national seat of government, Waller now prepared to offer members of the public their first opportunity to purchase lots in the city. Waller left no record of why he chose to hold the auction on the block bordered by Guadalupe, San Antonio, Pine (5th), and Cedar (4th) streets, but likely it was because this was one of the four public squares designated in his city plan. And the cluster of oak trees on the block's southwest corner would have offered welcoming shade in the summer heat.

For weeks leading up to this day, Waller had run an announcement of the auction in the Republic's newspapers.[2] Buyers therefore knew that a successful bid would require a down payment of at least 25 percent of the sale price, with three further installments due at six, 12, and 18 months. Waller would accept only gold, silver, government notes, or audited government paper as payment. That the government stood to reap a large profit on land obtained cheaply through the power of eminent domain had elicited charges of corruption from those opposed to situating the government on the western edge of Anglo settlement. Former President Sam Houston's booming voice reigned loudest in the crowd of critics assailing the move.[3]

Edwin Waller had studiously refrained from participating in the public debate about the sale. This was no doubt partly attributable to his own financial stake in the outcome, as his government contract allotted him a 5 percent commission on the day's proceeds. Auctioneer Doswell had struck an identical deal.[4]

Soon after the 10 AM start time, J. T. Doswell's gavel banged down in favor of M. H. Beaty's offer of $590 for the two lots comprising the southeast corner of the intersection of Mulberry (10th) and Rio Grande streets. Bidding closed hours later after Doswell had moved about 300 lots. Speculators played a large role in the bidding. Newspaper editor Samuel Whiting purchased 13 lots, while Louis P. Cooke, a member of the government commission that selected the land now being sold, bought eight. Nor did Waller and Doswell hold back, claiming six and two lots, respectively. The sale earned the cash-strapped Republic the enormous sum of $182,585, meaning that President Lamar's agent and auctioneer each cleared $9,129.25.[5]

Another government employee, surveyor L. J. Pilie, fared less well. Pilie drew the 1839 street plan that has since been reproduced in almost every book written about Austin. Together with

Charles Schoolfield, he also marked out the streets and building lot boundaries still in use. Having failed to acquire even a single lot, Pilie might have been forgiven for feeling a bit frustrated after the auction. What Edwin Waller and others could not forgive, however, was Pilie's theft of $3,500 that evening from J. T. Doswell. A quickly assembled jury led by Samuel Whiting declared Pilie guilty, after which the surveyor was tied to the "Liberty Pole," flogged, and exiled from Austin.[6]

VISIT THE SITE

- John Darlington's efforts notwithstanding, the block now known as Republic Square did not achieve permanent designation as a city park until the mid-1970s. As late as 1960 the land was being used as a parking lot. But the "Auction Oaks" survived, and the square is now undergoing revitalization by the Austin Parks Foundation. As it was in Edwin Waller's day, Republic Square is bounded by Guadalupe, San Antonio, 5th, and 4th streets. The Auction Oaks remain as one of the few landmarks within the original city limits present at Austin's founding. ❹

ENDNOTES

1. *Austin Statesman,* April 16, 1911.

2. *The Morning Star,* April 30, 1839.

3. This opposition continued even with the opening of the Fourth Congress, the first to convene in Austin, in 1839, when those opposed to Austin as the national capital introduced a bill to relocate the government. Speaking as the representative of San Augustine County, Sam Houston "commenced by alluding to the fraud which he said had been practised upon the members of the east, in the location at Austin." Amelia W. Williams

and Eugene C. Barker, eds., *The Writings of Sam Houston, 1813-1863,* vol. 2 (Austin: The University of Texas Press, 1939), p. 315.

4. Austin City Lots, Texas State Archives.

5. *Ibid.*

6. J. B. Ransom to Mirabeau Lamar, August 13, 1839. Charles Adams Gulick, Jr., ed., *The Papers of Mirabeau Buonaparte Lamar* (Austin: Texas State Library, 1922), item number 1402.

Auction Oaks in Republic Square. On August 1, 1839, Edwin Waller and James Doswell conducted the first public offering of Austin city lots in the shade of these trees.

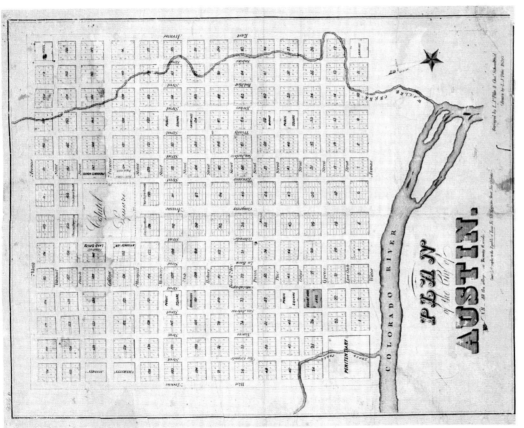

Street plan of Austin drawn in 1839 by L. J. Pilie.

7

LAMAR'S MANSION

"'There is the president's house,' said the driver, and looking up, we saw perched upon the top of one of the pinnacles of green, a white frame house."

—Julia Lee Sinks[1]

AUSTIN CITY PLANNER EDWIN WALLER wanted to place the permanent capitol building in the town's center. But topography dictated otherwise. As he studied the layout of the land he had to work with in 1839, Waller noticed that the dominant hill sat on the northern boundary. A broad ravine sliced directly from this gentle rise southward toward the river. Lesser prominences commanded the ravine, as well as the rest of the region, from either side. Scrapping his original idea, Waller reserved the largest hill to the north for the permanent capitol. He would build a temporary statehouse on the hill to the west of the ravine. The rise to the east seemed a perfect place for the house of the president. Pleased with himself, Waller wrote to President Mirabeau Lamar and remarked, "This selection of mine has been highly approved by all who have seen it and I doubt not will give universal satisfaction."[2]

Edwin Waller's block 85, soon to be known as "President's Hill," included the area bounded by Bois d'Arc (7th), San Jacinto, Hickory (8th), and Brazos streets. Originally a green peak suffused with wildflowers and lemon balm, the hill commanded a stunning view of the Colorado River valley. One early traveler saw his first buffalo on its grassy slopes. Another noted the clusters of oak trees grouped around its base.[3]

Edwin Waller had the house constructed with the view in mind. Its 54-foot length faced the river; large windows lined both floors. A stairwell in the central dogtrot greatly impressed one young visitor, who "climbed its giddy heights with fear and trembling."[4] Painters applied a coat of white paint to the entire structure, which as a result glistened in the sunlight and stirred pride in local residents.[5] Nor was this pride unjustified. A visiting reporter felt moved enough to write, "The president's house is the best building in the place . . . [It] appears almost a palace contrasted with the houses of the frontier hamlets."[6] Longtime resident William Walsh agreed that the mansion's "conspicuous" appearance pleased early citizens.[7] And future governor Francis Lubbock described President Lamar's home as "the most elegant looking building" in the city.[8]

Shy by nature and without a wife to serve as hostess, President Lamar mostly kept his new home private. He did, however, hold the occasional public ball. Julia Lee recalled attending one such event August 15, 1841.

The pathway up the hillside was thronged until the parlors were filled to overflowing. The young people flitted in and out and stood in merry groups around the hilltop, lapped in the soft, satiny folds of a Texas moonlight whose whiteness seemed almost palpable to the touch. What the infant republic lacked in house-room nature supplied, and to such fullness, with her breeze of balm and the downy softness of her moonbeams that no need of lordly halls was felt. In one of the post oaks in the yard two mocking birds were rivaling each other in melody, perhaps incited by the music of the dancers within and the music of merry voices without. In the distance, along the Colorado bottom the "Chick Will's Widow" sent up its mournful refrain to mingle with the other sounds of night, antiphonally answering the bursts of glee that bubbled and sparkled as if coming from fountain of eternal youth. Here, perhaps, some one was singing one of the popular songs of the times; there another group of two were [sic] talking in low, confidential tones not unlike the tale of love. Perhaps it was-who knows? Suddenly, amid the other sounds came the clattering of hoofs [sic] in the valley toward Waller creek. As their ears first caught the sound, there was a general uplifting of heads, a silent, listening pause, until the hoof beats seemed like the throbbing of an oppressed heart. "It is Indians," said several voices at once. Then was executed by the ladies what was known in Texas as a stampede. All at once there was a sudden breaking away from the beauties of the night. They flew to the house for shelter like a flock of pigeons, while the gentlemen lingered behind, listening for other advancing sounds, but hearing none, they, too, came in to answer eager questions. They reported "all quiet," and joy once more reinstated itself. We relate these trivial alarms to show how, mingled with all our mirth, were lurking the ever present undertones of probabilities, or at least possibilities. I will not call it the "bitter drop," because the frontier life would have been dull and flat without it.[9]

Within two years of Mirabeau Lamar's occupying his hilltop home, the structure was falling apart. In his haste to have everything ready for the government's arrival in 1839, Edwin Waller had been forced to use green lumber to construct the president's house. In December 1841, one newspaper editor observed that the building needed major repairs to "render it tenantable, which it, in its present condition, is not."[10] Incoming President Sam Houston certainly agreed. In notifying Congress that he would find other quarters he charged that, "The building itself is in a ruinous and dilapidated condition, and not in a situation to be tenanted with any degree of comfort to the occupant."[11]

Mirabeau Lamar was thus the only chief executive to occupy early Austin's finest edifice. An 1847 fire put the structure out of its misery by burning it to the ground. Julia Lee Sinks presaged the sad end with this recollection:

> We had walked to President hill, where as I write these last pages, the St. Mary's school stands, once occupied by the President's mansion, to gather some of those chalky daisies that grew there. Climbing the hillside among the tussocks of lemon balm, leaving the radiant scarlet phlox on the sandy slopes below, we stood on the gallery of the deserted and vacant house. . . . The spring winds sighed mournfully through the broken casements. No footprints, no signs of human life were to be seen.[12]

VISIT THE SITE

- What was once known as President's Hill is bounded by modern 7th, 8th, and Brazos streets, and San Jacinto Boulevard. Several feet of the hill were removed in 1954 with the demolition of St. Mary's Academy. Since 1986 the Austin Centre, a 16-story office and hotel building, has covered the entire city block. To obtain a hint of the original view enjoyed by Mirabeau Lamar, stand on either corner of the block and look south toward the river. ❻

ENDNOTES

1. Julia Lee Sinks, *Early Days in Texas: Reminiscences of Julia Lee Sinks,* Julia Lee Sinks vertical file, Barker Center for American History, The University of Texas at Austin.

2. Roxanne Kuter Williamson, *Austin, Texas: An American Architectural History* (San Antonio, Trinity University Press, 1973), p. 11.

3. A. B. Lawrence, *Texas in 1840, Or The Emigrant's Guide to the New Republic* (Austin: W.M. Morrison Books, 1987, reprint of the original edition printed in New York in 1840), p. 61.

4. *Austin Statesman,* January 27, 1924.

5. Julia Lee Sinks wrote, ". . . its white front, with its upper and lower porticoes, glittered in the sun, the green of the hill lying below, making a soft, shadowy contrast to its brilliancy, and this same sun with its warmth seeming to enter our hearts, made us look up loyally and feel that the house was good enough for a king."

6. *Telegraph and Texas Register,* December 11, 1839.

7. *Austin Statesman,* January 27, 1924.

8. Francis Richard Lubbock, *Six Decades in Texas,* ed. by C.W. Raines (Austin: Ben C. Jones & Company Printers, 1900), p. 143.

9. Julia Lee Sinks, *Early Days in Texas: Reminiscences of Julia Lee Sinks,* Julia Lee Sinks vertical file, Barker Center for American History, The University of Texas at Austin.

10. *Austin City Gazette,* December 1, 1841.

11. Report to Congress Concerning the Condition of the President's Residence, December 23, 1841. Amelia W. Williams and Eugene C. Barker, eds., *The Writings of Sam Houston, 1813-1863,* vol. 2 (Austin: The University of Texas Press, 1939), pp. 409-410.

12. Julia Lee Sinks, *Early Days in Texas: Reminiscences of Julia Lee Sinks,* Julia Lee Sinks vertical file, Barker Center for American History, The University of Texas at Austin.

Mirabeau Lamar's 1839 Presidential Mansion sat here on one of the highest spots within the original city limits. Construction of this office and hotel complex involved removing about 10-15 feet of the hill's elevation.

This view south from the site of Lamar's presidential mansion still yields a commanding view of lower downtown Austin.

8

LAMAR'S FOLLY

"HOW WELL I REMEMBER THE CRUNCHING of gravel as we passed up the walk," recalled Julia Lee, in her early twenties at the time of her first visit to the frontier capitol of the Republic of Texas.[1] Julia and her companions had risked walking through a moonless Austin night to cross the wooden bridge spanning the moat outside the stockade surrounding the building. But the excitement of a dance party beckoned, and as they approached the south end of the Senate chamber they delighted at "a soft and beautiful" melody spilling through the open windows, accompanied by the "peculiar voice" of the violinist, a man named Smithson, calling out the dance.

Inside the Senate chamber, Julia marveled at the elegant dress of the ladies in attendance, which seemed so incongruous with the room's crude appearance and, for that matter, the city's itself. During a break in the music someone dressed a Mexican man in an "Indian war suit" captured during a recent skirmish. The faux warrior strode boldly down the length of the room "for the shuddering delight of the ladies." Behind him strode two authentic warriors, both of whom had participated in the fight. Captain

Mark Lewis came first, receiving warm greetings from those in the crowd. Behind him followed Flacco, a Lipan Apache thought by Julia to be "the truest friend that Texas ever had among the red men."

Flacco smiled broadly as he passed among the Anglos, shaking an extended hand with whoever would accept it. Julia "touched it with fear, mingled with feelings near akin to repugnance . . . ." Despite her prejudices, she noted that the man she regarded as having sprung from among savages, possessed "the stamp of true nobleness." Julia commented of Flacco years later that "[f]rom among the many known Indians, not one spark of the chivalry of romance was ever detected except in this instance."

The dance attended by Julia Lee was held in the Senate chamber, which occupied the north end of the 60 x 110-foot capitol building. The larger House chamber occupied the south end, with a dogtrot separating the two rooms. Lining the back (western) side of the building were seven small committee rooms. A covered porch spanned the entire front, while chimneys protruded from either end. Builder Benjamin Noble employed rough cedar to construct the frame, which he covered with sawed pine planks from Bastrop. A coat of white paint gave the structure a more dignified appearance than most other buildings in Austin at the time.[2]

With his arrival at what was to become Austin in May 1839, government agent Edwin Waller set to work immediately to erect what would be the most crucial government building in town. This may explain why the finished capitol complex did not conform to the street grid eventually established. Waller also wanted to take advantage of the hill lying just west of Congress Avenue in the vicinity of Hickory (8th) Street. Not a year earlier President Mirabeau Lamar had killed an enormous buffalo at the base of this rise.[3] Situated atop the hill, Waller's capitol building complimented the similarly elevated presidential mansion located a block east of Congress Avenue. These two structures therefore dominated the entire town.

Facing Congress Avenue from its hilltop perch, the original Austin capitol nevertheless sat well back of that thoroughfare. About 60 feet behind the capitol was a smaller building, 20 x 70 feet with kitchen, dining room, a few beds, and a tiny room stocked with "refreshments." One contemporary later wrote, "I don't know whether these were described as 'contingent expenses' or were sold as articles of commerce, but the business was generally good."[4] Teetotalers could quench their thirst at one of two wells dug between the refreshment room and main building, a spot now occupied by Colorado Street.

One feature of the complex congruent with the notion of a frontier capitol building seems to have been added as an afterthought. Ever fearful of Indian attack, city residents erected a palisade of upright hewn logs around the buildings, then dug a three-foot deep trench around this. Not everyone appreciated the effort and some even ridiculed it. A spoof in the *Austin City Gazette* included this verse:

> I'm sure Lamar thinks it is right
> To save the public archives—
> Then tell me, vot's so snug and tight
> As rough logs stuck up endvies?[5]

In that same edition was a report of someone having "fill[ed] the big guns in 'Lamar's Folly' with stones."[6] But if some pranksters laughed at the building's usefulness as a fortress, other residents took the idea quite seriously. The famed Twin Sisters cannons[7] took up residence there, while one visitor wrote home of seeing "large piles of muskets, Balls, and Bombshells . . . ."[8]

Given the scarcity of large buildings in early Austin, the capitol offered itself as a natural meeting place for city residents. Julia Lee Sinks recalled years later that, for an unknown reason, the Senate chamber saw more use than its partner. "It was not only the public forum for all oratorical display, whether religious or political," she wrote, "but it was the theater of our greatest social events and pleasant reunions."[9] At one 1840 church service Vice President David Burnet's son was baptized.[10] Edward Fontaine, who later was instrumental in the founding of St. David's Episcopal Church, spoke at another. Still another saw an appearance by a nephew of author Washington Irving.[11]

Any man deemed worthy of public honor found himself being toasted in a decorated Senate chamber. A dinner for Colonel William Cooke, leader of an expedition charged with opening a road to the Red River, triggered one such rush by Austin's women to spruce up what was otherwise a very plain room. Stacks of polished muskets festooned the hall, which was lit by chandeliers of bayonets dangling from the ceiling. Unsheathed swords hung on walls to form the outline of the Texas star. A Mexican flag captured at San Jacinto fluttered from the ceiling. The ladies even decorated themselves by wearing wreaths of greenery to complement their white dresses.[12]

School teacher Sarah Humphries hosted a less martial affair in the Senate when she organized a May celebration "for the pleasure of the children and the delight of the mothers." Miss Humphries' class was the only one in Austin at the time, a fact implying that every mother in town[13] would have participated. Although the event's activities are now forgotten, "the wild flowers of Texas figured freely in the scene and made glad the day."[14]

Ironically, the man who fought most vigorously against placing the Texas government in Austin is also the only Texas president to have been inaugurated in the city.[15] Late in the morning of December 13, 1841, Sam Houston took the oath of office in a ceremony held at the capitol's rear entrance.[16] The flamboyant Houston had ordered a green velvet suit and hat from France for the occasion but, perhaps in deference to his more conservative wife Margaret, left them at home in favor of standard dress. New technology nevertheless introduced a dramatic flair to the ceremony. Telegraph wires had been run between the capitol and the arsenal[17] so that, at the precise moment of the swearing in, a signal from an observer triggered a booming artillery salute in the distance. As was his habit, President Houston then seized the opportunity of delivering a lengthy speech.

Perhaps the most poignant official ceremony involving the old capitol took place February 19, 1846, when President Anson Jones formally acknowledged the end of the Republic of Texas. The first state legislature had convened three days earlier, meaning that the republic had already ceased to exist. But, according to bystander Noah Smithwick, this fact only hit home with the lowering of the Texas flag in favor of the stars and stripes. Hundreds of people packed the hillside in front of the capitol to witness President Jones say,

The lone star of Texas, which ten years since arose amid clouds over fields of carnage and obscurely shone for a while, has culminated, and, following an inscrutable destiny, has passed on and become fixed forever in that glorious constellation which all freemen and lovers of freedom in the world must reverence and adore—the American Union.

Jones then hauled down the Texas flag, folded it, and uttered to a silent crowd,

The final act in this great drama is now performed. The republic of Texas is no more.[18]

As he did so "many a head was bowed, many a broad chest heaved, and many a manly cheek was wet with tears . . . ." But, with the appearance of the American flag,

A mighty cheer went up, hats were thrown high, a cannon boomed and there was a tremendous tumult. Never before and never since have I seen such a sudden change from grief to rejoicing. It was marvelous.[19]

Never intended for more than a few years of service, Austin's original capitol building survived only until 1857, when it was demolished and its land donated to the city for a market house and city hall. One contemporary report noted that,

One by one the vestiges of our former nationality disappear. To the old Texian these things produce a sorrowful impression, despite the conviction that they are the results of time and progress. He cannot forget the day when this humble house was the capitol of a nation few in numbers, but rich in the elements of patriotism—blindly and ardently devoted to the country, and ever ready with stout hands and brave hearts to defend it . . . The old house is gone-it has disappeared before the resistless wave of progress—it is numbered with the things that were; yet there are loyal hearts which will beat faster when they think of the by-gone days when it was the capitol of a fearless people.[20]

VISIT THE SITE

- The first temporary capitol in Austin faced east and occupied lots 9, 10, and 11 of block 98 of Edwin Waller's original Austin city plan. Lots 7 through 12 fronted the eastern side of Colorado Street from north to south between 9th (formerly Ash) and 8th (formerly Hickory) streets. A well behind the capitol sat in what is now Colorado Street. Since the two wells on the grounds were said to lie between the capitol and the "retiring room," the latter structure must have been situated on the present northwest corner of the intersection of Colorado and 8th streets. ❺

ENDNOTES

1. Details of this episode are from Julia Lee Sinks, *Early Days in Texas,* comp. by Frances Brady Underwood (Austin: Nortex Press, 2005), pp. 26-30.

2. Details of the 1839 capitol's construction are from William Walsh's recollections, which appeared in the January 27, 1924, edition of the *Austin Statesman* and Roxanne Kuter Williamson, *Austin, Texas: An American Architectural History* (San Antonio, Trinity University Press, 1973), p. 14.

3. At what is now the intersection of Congress Avenue and 8th Street. Alex W. Terrell, "The City of Austin From 1839 to 1865," vol. 014, no. 2, *Southwestern Historical Quarterly Online,* pp. 113-128. http://www.tsha.utexas.edu/publicatons/journals/shq/online/v014/n2/article_2.html.

4. *Austin Statesman,* January 27, 1924.

5. *Austin City Gazette,* May 13, 1840.

6. *Ibid.*

7. The Twin Sisters were a pair of artillery pieces presented to the Texas army by the citizens of Cincinnati during the Texas Revolution which arrived just in time to see action at the Battle of San Jacinto.

8. George Grover to Charles Grover, June 17, 1840, Texas State Archives.

9. Sinks, p. 44.

10. A. B. Lawrence, *Texas in 1840, Or the Emigrant's Guide to the New Republic* (Austin: W.M. Morrison Books, 1987, first printed in New York, 1840), pp. 66-67.

11. Sinks, pp. 44-45.

12. *Ibid.,* pp. 46-47.

13. Every white mother, that is. An 1840 census by Presbyterian minister Amos Roark showed that 17% of Austin's population consisted of black slaves, who were excluded from such activities. Frank Brown, *Annals of Travis County and the City of Austin,* Chap. Austin History Center: Austin, Texas.

14. Sinks, p. 48.

15. Successor Anson Jones, the Republic's last President, took the oath of office in Washington (now called Washington-on-the-Brazos).

16. Details of the inauguration ceremony are from the *Daily Bulletin,* December 13, 1841, as quoted in the Austin File Chronological, Item 2, 1841, Austin: Austin History Center.

17. The arsenal occupied the block formed by East Avenue and Water (Cesar Chavez), Sabine, and Live Oak (2nd) streets.

18. Stephen B. Oates, ed., *Rip Ford's Texas* (Austin: University of Texas Press, 2004), p 56.

19. These are remarks of William Henry Stewart, later a Texas legislator and mayor of Gonzales. A. C. Greene, "End of Texas Republic Marked by Sadness, Joy [Texas Sketches]," *Dallas Morning News,* October 13, 1996.

20. Anson Jones, *Memoranda and Official Correspondence Relating to the Republic of Texas-Its History and Annexation 1836 to 1846* (Chicago: The Rio Grande Press, Inc., 1966, reprint of the original 1859 edition), pp. 603-604.

The first Texas capitol in Austin occupied the ground now covered by the old City Hall building seen at left in this photograph.

Looking north along Colorado Street at its intersection with 8th (Hickory) Street. Sam Houston's second presidential inauguration occured here at the back of the capitol building.

Looking north from 8th (Hickory) Street between Colorado Street and Congress Avenue. The 1839 capitol building faced Congress Avenue from this location

When the 1839 capitol was razed in 1857, the state donated the land to Austin as a site for a new City Hall and market house. The current building dates to 1905, although extensive remodeling in the 1930's drastically altered its outward appearance.

9

BULLOCK'S FORT[1]

ONE BEAUTIFUL SPRING DAY IN 1840 Julia Lee, a new immigrant from Ohio, sat in a wagon rumbling into Austin via the road from Montopolis. Accompanied by her sister and two brothers, young Miss Lee delighted in the abundant prairie wildflowers blanketing the landscape. A sweet fragrance of rye grass and pollen heightened her pleasure. Glistening moisture from a brief spring shower transformed the roadway into a "valley of diamonds." As fears of Indian attack ebbed, Lee and her siblings rejoiced that they had arrived safely in the "city of the hills."[2]

The excited newcomers stopped first at the Thompson House[3] but were turned away for lack of room. A ride of four blocks west and two blocks south brought them to the busiest intersection in town at Congress Avenue and Pecan (6th) Street. There they secured lodging from Austin's first landlords, Richard and Mary Bullock. The Lees didn't know it, but they had stumbled into the social and political hub of the Republic's capital.

Richard and Mary Bullock were among Austin's first residents in 1839. Whether by astuteness or good fortune the couple quickly began construction of a hotel in what was to become the city's commercial heart. One suspects the former, considering the main road into Austin at that time entered from the east to meet up with Pecan Street. The Bullock property along the south side of Pecan on the west side of its intersection with Congress Avenue, which was certainly intended as a major thoroughfare, could not have been situated more ideally.

Richard Bullock began construction of his hotel even before Edwin Waller's surveyors had finished laying out Austin's streets. He first erected a log house at the corner of the alley and West Pecan Street.[4] Next came extensions, also out of hewn logs, eastward along Pecan, northward along the alley, and eastward along the lot's north line, to form a courtyard opening towards Congress. Numerous oaks and elm trees shaded those relaxing in this open space. Cool water was at hand from the well. Adjacent to the easternmost log house on Pecan Street, Bullock placed a log house raised up by tall posts. Austin residents joked about the building's ungainliness. Julia Lee recalled one woman remarking, "[it] looked like it was frightened, and wanted to run away."[5] Bullock soon enclosed the area underneath the log house with weatherboarding to create the hotel's dining room. He completed construction by placing a log house in the center of the courtyard for use as a parlor. The imposing nature of the complex soon had Austin residents referring to "Bullock's Fort," an appropriate appellation once an 18-pound artillery piece was moved onto the grounds.

Many early Austin dignitaries enjoyed Richard and Mary Bullock's hospitality. Sam Houston resided in the two-story building closest to the Avenue during his stint in the Fourth Congress.

Physician Richard Brenham[6] occupied a room on Pecan Street. Secretary of State Abner Lipscomb and Supreme Court Chief Justice John Hemphill were tenants, as was R. E. B. Baylor, judge and the person for whom Baylor University is named. Count Alphonse de Saligny of Pig War fame was a guest.[7] In all, Bullock's housed about 60 or 70 people at any one time. As Julia Lee noted, "It sheltered all ministers, both spiritual and temporal, all negotiators with the government, all judicial dignitaries, all heroes of the nation, whether civil or military, all army and navy aspirants. All that sought dignity or assumed dignity in any form found and shared its inviting hospitality . . . . It was the home to all, as I have said before, who came to Austin either for business or curiosity."[8]

Bullock's quickly became a central gathering place, even for non-tenants. A jumble of logs left over from construction on Congress Avenue attracted passersby with enough regularity that Austinites dubbed the spot "Loafer's Logs." Regulars included a survivor of the Goliad massacre named John Holiday, Santa Fe Expedition leader Hugh McLeod, and Richard Brenham. A jug of whiskey often made the rounds as the men swapped stories and jokes. A humorous circular labeled *The Austin Spy* mysteriously appeared on occasion, left behind by its anonymous author to be found and read aloud for the crowd's pleasure.

Mary Bullock provided a more refined form of public entertainment. Her piano was likely the first in Austin. Guests gathered in her parlor to hear her play and sing such songs as "Not a Gun Was Heard," "The Minute Gun at Sea," and "The Carrier Dove." Guests and locals alike also enjoyed browsing in her "china room," which occupied a cabin on the north side of the complex. Its shelves displayed not only a complete tea service and breakfast and dinner set but an extensive collection of ceramics from France.

The parlor also provided refuge from threatened Indian attack. Frightened women and children cowered for hours while waiting for the alarm to be lifted. Fear often gave way to boredom, which in turn led to attempts at humor or song by the stouter of heart. Some even tried to dance. Such efforts elicited cries of admonishment from those whose concern had not yet dissipated. Any man in the shelter sought to soothe the crowd's fears. Julia Lee recalled George Hockley's[9] strolling among them while cooing, "Don't get frightened, ladies, don't get frightened; there are enough men here to whip all the Indians between here and Santa Fe."[10]

As one of the largest rooms in the city,[11] Richard and Mary Bullock's dining hall witnessed many a public gathering in early Austin. Residents gathered there in 1840 to enjoy a Fourth of July feast prepared by Mary Bullock. But the social highlight of the hotel's existence had occurred the previous fall with the arrival of President Mirabeau Lamar in the city he had helped create.

Lamar's dream of expanding the Texan empire turned on diverting to the Texas coast the rich trade between the United States and Mexico that passed through Santa Fe. He envisioned a great frontier metropolis capable of receiving overland goods from Santa Fe, transferring them to boats, and floating them down the Colorado to ships waiting to sail to New Orleans and beyond. Once in office, he lobbied successfully for a western seat of government. The result was this new city of Austin.

Lamar's many detractors included his predecessor, the powerful Sam Houston. Houston and others ridiculed the practicality of building a city on the edge of Anglo civilization. Once construction had begun in May 1839, Lamar's opponents scoffed at the notion that the city would be ready to receive the Fourth Congress that fall. Yet Lamar's agent Edwin Waller pulled off the miracle, and in October wagons loaded with government archives began rumbling out of Houston toward the new government seat.

Mirabeau Lamar celebrated his triumph October 17, 1839, when Edwin Waller and other dignitaries met him two miles east of town. After speeches and a welcoming cannon blast, Lamar led the procession across East Avenue before following Pecan Street to Congress Avenue. At 3 o'clock the president took his place at the head of the table in Mary and Richard Bullock's dining hall for Austin's first formal dinner. Emcee James Burke toasted the guest of honor, after which Lamar rose and thanked Edwin Waller with the remark, "By the touch of his industry there has sprung up, like the work of magic, a beautiful city, whose glory is destined, in a few years, to overshadow the ancient magnificence of Mexico."[12]

Less than three years later Richard Bullock was dead, a victim of fever on the road between Galveston and Austin. His widow married one of her former tenants, Abner Lipscomb, in 1843. James Swisher built a two-story hotel in 1849 that filled in the open space between Bullock's and Congress Avenue. At about that same time Swisher acquired the Bullock property. Swisher's Hotel became Smith Hotel in 1858 and Cook's Hotel in 1861 after being acquired by master builder Abner Cook. By the 1870's the edifice was showing enough age that the *Daily Democratic Statesman* opined, "The order of the day is to pull down all shabby barns in the business part of the city and replace them with handsome buildings. In view of this we assume Colonel Cook will get rid of the old bat roost on the corner of the Avenue and Pecan Street."[13] Cook dallied for another two years after reading this, but in August 1875 the building came down.[14]

VISIT THE SITE

- Bullock's Hotel sat on lot 1 of block 70 as numbered on Edwin Waller's 1839 plan for Austin. This lot was bounded by Congress Avenue, Pecan (6th) Street, lot 2 immediately to the north, and the north-south alley bisecting the entire block. It spanned 46 feet of the west side of Congress Avenue and 160 feet of the north side of Pecan Street. The complex sat far enough back from Congress Avenue that James Swisher was able to place his two story hotel between it and the Avenue in 1849. One American Center, a 32-story office building, has covered most of the city block since 1984. ❾

ENDNOTES

1. Most of the information about Bullock's Hotel presented here is derived from Frank Brown, *Annals of Travis County and the City of Austin, Chapter VI,* Austin History Center, Austin, Texas, and Julia Lee Sinks, *Reminiscences of Julia Lee Sinks,* Julia Lee Sinks vertical file, Barker Center for American History, The University of Texas at Austin.

2. Julia Lee Sinks, comp. Frances Brady Underwood, *Early Days in Texas* (Austin: Nortex Press, 2005), p. 9.

3. W. W. Thompson's hotel on the northeast corner of the intersection of Hickory (8th) and Neches streets. *Texas National Register,* December 17, 1845, and *Texas Democrat,* March 20, 1847.

4. The alley for this city block, bounded by Congress Avenue, Pecan (6th), Bois d'Arc (7th), and Colorado streets, ran parallel to Congress Avenue and divided the block into two equal portions.

5. Sinks, p. 12.

6. Brenham participated in the Santa Fe Expedition and the Mier Expedition. He was killed in 1843 with the latter. The town of Brenham is named in his honor.

7. See the chapter "The Pig War."

8. Sinks, p. 12.

9. A close friend of Sam Houston, Hockley commanded the artillery at the Battle of San Jacinto. He was also Secretary of War during both of Houston's presidential administrations.

10. Sinks, page 14.

11. The House and Senate chambers in the Capitol building two blocks north were also available. Julia Lee Sinks recalled that, for an unknown reason, the Senate chamber was used more often.

12. *Austin City Gazette,* October 30, 1839.

13. *Daily Democratic Statesman,* April 26, 1873.

14. Kenneth Hafertepe, *Abner Cook: Master Builder on the Texas Frontier* (Austin: Texas State Historical Association, 1992), p. 169.

Looking west along 6th (Pecan) Street at Congress Avenue. Richard and Mary Bullock's hotel complex stretched along the north side of Pecan Street between Congress and Colorado Street one block to the west.

10

THE EBERLY HOUSE

TO HIS DYING DAY SAM HOUSTON denied responsibility, but many of his contemporaries blamed him for the 1836 burning of San Felipe de Austin,[1] at the time one of the more prosperous cities in Texas. Austin hotel owner Angelina Eberly left no record of her feelings on the matter, but surely she held an opinion, and likely a strong one, for her San Felipe establishment had gone up in flames with the rest of the town. What thoughts coursed through her mind then as she prepared to host a party for the man whom she might well have blamed for her earlier loss?

Angelina Eberly's life story is a tale of resilience.[2] After marrying Jonathan Peyton and residing for a time in Tennessee, the former Angelina Bell moved with her husband to Matagorda by way of New Orleans in 1822. A series of moves brought the couple to San Felipe de Austin in 1825. There Jonathan met Stephen F. Austin, from whom he secured a land grant in 1827, making him one of Austin's original "Old Three Hundred" land recipients. The Peytons also purchased several lots in San Felipe. On one of these they erected a tavern to be run by Angelina.

An unknown illness carried Jonathan off in 1834, leaving Angelina to provide for herself and two children. She was anything but destitute, however, owning eight slaves, four town lots, the tavern, and several other buildings in San Felipe at the time of her husband's death. That she may not have been a stellar tavern hostess is implied by a comment from one of her San Felipe boarders, future Texas president Mirabeau Lamar, who recorded in his journal, "Arrived at San Philippe Wednesday 9th Septr. Staid [sic] a day or two at Johnson's tavern; but fairing [sic] badly, I re-moved to Mrs. Peyton's and fared a great deal worse."[3]

March 1836 unleashed the dogs of war on San Felipe and the Widow Peyton. Convinced that his rebel army was not yet prepared to face the disciplined troops of Mexican President Santa Anna, General Sam Houston began an eastward retreat. Panicked settlers packed what they could and began an exodus now known as the Runaway Scrape. As refugees streamed through San Felipe in one direction, the Liberty County company led by Captain William Logan passed through in the other. Company member N. D. Labadie recalled Angelina Peyton and a group of women standing in front of her tavern "[giving] us repeated cheers, waving their handkerchiefs incessantly as we left."[4]

Not long thereafter, General Houston arrived at San Felipe, where many of his men expected to make a stand at the Brazos River town. The following morning, however, the commander gave the order to resume the march. Captains Moseley Baker and Wiley Martin refused. Rather than risk losing even more men by attempting to force compliance in an atmosphere of discontent, Houston *ordered* Martin downriver to protect a key crossing point and Baker to defend the crossing at San Felipe. Realizing that, at best, Captain Baker's men would only be able to delay the Mexican advance through their town, San Felipe residents joined the eastward stream of refugees. Baker's men indeed succeeded in momentarily halting Santa Anna but faced with overwhelming numerical disadvantage pulled out to join the retreat. Before leaving, though, Baker had his men set the town ablaze in order to deprive the Mexicans of its store of goods, Mrs. Peyton's buildings burning with the rest. Baker later claimed that he had been ordered by Houston to destroy San Felipe.[5] Although Houston vigorously denied giving any such order, many contemporaries believed Baker's claim. Whether Angelina was a member of this group is unknown.

The now homeless widow landed in Columbia, where she met and married a widower named Jacob Eberly. It is not clear how Angelina occupied herself for the next three years, but in 1839 she and her husband left Columbia for the frontier government seat of Austin being constructed on the Colorado River. At the first public sale of city lots, Angelina purchased three of her own on the northeast corner of West Pecan (6th) and Lavaca streets.[6] There she erected the Eberly House, one of the first hotels in the city.

Angelina's poor luck with husbands continued when Jacob died in May 1841. Yet the hotel prospered, and in December of that same year the twice-widowed hostess bustled about the premises in preparation for the arrival of the nation's president-elect. A large party of excited citizens met the dignitary east of town and escorted him to quarters at the Eberly House. And thus, Angelina offered greetings to Sam Houston, the man many still blamed for the torching of her former home. Either she held no grudge or kept her feelings to herself, judging from Houston's happy report to his wife that "On yesterday I rec'd the most elegant and hearty greeting that I have ever done."[7]

Lodging was scarce in frontier Austin, and even the president-elect had to share his room at the Eberly House.[8]

On the morning of December 13, 1841, the Travis Guards arrived at the hotel to escort Sam Houston to the capitol, where he took the presidential oath of office. Afterwards the President treated both houses of Congress to refreshments at Mrs. Eberly's.[9]

Bitter political enemies Sam Houston and Mirabeau Lamar agreed on very little, but the former echoed the words of the latter in his judgment of Mrs. Eberly's skills as an innkeeper. In a letter to his wife, Houston complained, "I am just ready to ride out this evening and get a morsel to eat, for here my love I can get nothing fit to live on. Indeed I would pity a dog who was situated as I am. I have no bed to sleep upon."[10] Evidently he found little to his liking even around town, for just a few days later he observed, "Poor dear Wives, but they have a sad time, if it is only half as bad as that of their husbands in Austin. Why my Love, you can, in Houston, obtain something to eat. Some oysters, some fruit, or some bread that is palatiable [sic], but here we are destitute and miserable in mind as well as body."[11]

In 1842 Sam Houston, never fond of Austin as the capital, seized upon the threat posed by two separate Mexican army incursions as far north as San Antonio to move the government to Washington.[12] Defiant Austin residents refused to part with the records of the land office, however, and in December Houston dispatched a detail to sneak the archives out of town. All went well until several people, including Angelina Eberly, noticed the suspicious activity at the land office. A nearby cannon was rolled into Congress Avenue where someone, perhaps Angelina, touched off the piece to warn the town of the threat. Houston's detachment made it as far as Brushy Creek, where angry city residents forced the return of the archives. Then, in a move that might have seemed like ironic justice to Angelina, the records were sealed in tin boxes, taken to the Eberly House, and buried for safekeeping.[13]

VISIT THE SITE

- The Eberly House occupied lots 1, 2, and 3 of block 71 in downtown Austin, which is bounded by Lavaca, Colorado, 6th, and 7th streets. The three lots make up the southwest quadrant of this block. ❽

ENDNOTES

1. According to San Jacinto veteran N. D. Labadie, shortly after San Felipe burned, Houston asked him and another man if they had ever heard him order the destruction of the town. When Labadie's companion answered in the negative, Houston said, "Yet they blame me for it." Eugene C. Barker, "The San Jacinto Campaign." *Southwestern Historical Quarterly,* vol. 4, no. 5, p. 310.

2. Many of the details of Angelina Eberly's life presented here are from L. W. Kemp, "Mrs. Angelina Eberly." *Southwestern Historical Quarterly,* vol. 36, no. 3, pp. 193-199.

3. Mirabeau Buonaparte Lamar, *Mirabeau B. Lamar Travel Journal, 1835* (June–October, 1835), p. 179.

4. Kemp, p. 195.

5. Baker stated that Houston "gave me orders to burn the town on the approach of the enemy." Barker, p. 279.

6. Austin City Lots, Texas State Archives.

7. Madge Thornall Roberts, ed., *The Personal Correspondence of Sam Houston, vol. 1, 1839-1845* (Denton: University of North Texas Press, 1996), p. 123.

8. *Ibid.,* p. 132.

9. Francis Richard Lubbock, *Six Decades in Texas* (Austin: Ben C. Jones & Co. Printers, 1900), p. 142.

10. Roberts, p. 181.

11. *Ibid.,* p. 196.

12. We now refer to this town as Washington-on-the-Brazos, but in 1842 it was merely called Washington.

13. See the chapter "Stealing Back the Archives."

Northeast view at Lavaca and 6th (Pecan) streets. The Eberly House sat on the northeast corner of this intersection, a site now occupied by Claudia Taylor Johnson Hall (formerly a United States Post Office).

11

THE SUNDAY SCHOOL MAN

FRONTIER TEXAS EARNED A WELL-DESERVED reputation as a destination of scoundrels and thieves. Many early settlers sought not only economic opportunity but a chance to escape creditors, lawmen, or an unsavory past. Their number included some of the most legendary of Texas heroes, including Alamo defenders William Barret Travis and Jim Bowie.[1] But where sinners go, pious men wanting to save them follow. One of those pious men was South Carolina-born James Burke.

Presbyterian Burke sold a profitable business in Natchez, Mississippi, before moving to San Augustine, Texas, in 1837. Soon thereafter he moved to Houston, where in March 1839 the Reverend W. Y. Allen named Burke ruling elder of the new Presbyterian Church he was organizing. Five months later Burke successfully bid on several lots in the new seat of government being constructed on the Colorado River by Edwin Waller. In October 1839 he escorted Reverend Allen from Bastrop to Austin, where Allen again named Burke elder of a new Presbyterian congregation, the first in the city. Burke's strong religious faith became well enough known that Austin residents took to calling him the "Sunday School Man."

James Burke brought a strong literary interest as well as his faith to Texas. Shortly after his 1837 arrival he gained a position as assistant House clerk in the Second Congress. This vantage point enabled him to publish a newsletter of congressional activity. The paper was the first to appear daily in Texas.

Upon moving to Austin, Burke also opened a mercantile business at Congress Avenue and Bois d'Arc (7th) Street. He owned the two lots making up the south side of Bois d'Arc between Congress and Colorado Street, as well as the adjacent lot fronting Congress Avenue.[2] Burke sold the usual line of dry goods, which for Austin store owners at that time consisted of whatever they could obtain from Houston. In addition, prospective travelers were invited to the store to purchase tickets on Thomas Marler's newly established stage line between Austin and Houston.[3]

James Burke planned on supporting himself with his store but displayed one of his passions by announcing a public reading room adjacent to the business. He planned on stocking all newspapers printed in Texas and as many from the United States as he could procure. Eventually, a lending library would also be established. Congressmen in particular were invited to avail themselves of Burke's offer, but everyone was welcome. The room would contain "all the facilities and conveniences usually connected with such establishments," whatever those might be.[4]

James Burke's reading room debuted Monday, November 11, 1839. Tragically for the Sunday School Man, only days later his building became the first structure in Austin to be destroyed by fire. Bystanders rushed to save the store's merchandise but could not prevent the flames from consuming everything else. A notice in the *Austin City Gazette* lamented Burke's loss, not only for his sake, but for "the great want of buildings at the moment."[5]

An undaunted Burke vowed to rebuild. In the meantime, he somehow managed to re-open his mercantile business (minus the reading room) among the ashes of what he now called "Phoenix Corner."[6] What business he attracted, however, proved insufficient. Only a few weeks later, in January 1840, Burke offered to sell the property, with its three rooms fronting Congress Avenue and "comfortable" log house on Bois d'Arc.[7] Phoenix Corner would rise no more.

VISIT THE SITE

- James Burke owned the north side of West 7th Street between Congress Avenue and Colorado Street, as well as the adjacent lot on Congress. The corner lot facing Congress is now home to the Sampson Henricks Building (1859), the oldest on the Avenue. Come at mealtime to enjoy Thai food in the restaurant occupying the first floor. ❼

ENDNOTES

1. Travis abandoned a son and pregnant wife in Alabama, while Bowie left Louisiana after his scheme to sell fraudulent land titles unraveled.

2. *Texas Sentinel,* February 12, 1840. This edition contains a notice by Burke offering those three lots for sale.

3. *Austin City Gazette,* November 27, 1839.

4. *Ibid.* November 4, 1839.

5. *Ibid.* November 20, 1839.

6. *Ibid.* November 27, 1839.

7. *Texas Sentinel,* February 12, 1840.

Southwest view at Congress Avenue and 7th (Bois d'Arc) Street. James Burke owned the land now occupied by the 1859 Sampson-Henricks Building, as well as the adjacent Congress Avenue lot.

12

THE SAGA OF VIRGINIA WEBSTER[1]

IN MARCH 1840 A MAN NAMED Cooksey escorted Jane Webster and her two young children into a San Antonio building to view the bodies of several dead Indians. The room they entered had been the scene of a disastrous prisoner exchange between Republic of Texas forces and the Comanche. When Comanche leader Mukwahruh showed up with only one Anglo captive, 16-year-old Matilda Lockhart, and several Mexican children, the Texans, including Hugh McLeod and William Cooke, informed their guests that the Indians were now hostages. The enraged Comanche reached for their weapons. Minutes later dozens lay dead, with the Comanche suffering the greater loss.[2]

Cooksey shuddered at the sight that greeted the party. Deep red blood darkened the floor while bits of flesh and tissue clung to the walls. The 4-year-old girl in his arms, however, remained calm. As Cooksey carried her about the room, young Virginia pointed here and there, calling several of the dead Comanche by name. Cooksey marveled at her demeanor, later calling her the "nerviest" child he had ever met.[3]

Surprised as he was by Virginia Webster's coolness, Cooksey had expected her to recognize some of the corpses. Days earlier Virginia, along with her mother and brother, had stumbled upon a caravan of Mexican traders about three miles from town. Jane explained to the incredulous men that they had escaped from the Comanche after a year-long captivity. Their ordeal had begun during a journey to a new home on the North San Gabriel River. But before they could reach their destination, the Websters encountered a different fate on a road near present-day Austin.

Unlike many who came to Texas in the 1830's, John Webster was not a poor man, but a Virginia plantation owner seeking to make even greater riches in a new land of opportunity. After selling his Potomac River land and all but 10 of his 110 slaves, he opened a bank in Wheeling and moved his family to a nearby farm in Harrison County. A sawmill, gristmill, and store would supplement his earnings. Texas beckoned, though, and in 1836 Webster sold most of his property, left $10,000 in the Wheeling bank, and headed south. He brought not only his family and a few slaves but a company of 44 men lured by his tales of potential wealth.

Webster and his party landed at Galveston in November 1836. His plan for self-enrichment involved land speculation. Among the group of men was a surveyor; the others were along to provide manual labor and protection against Indians. Military service would provide the means of obtaining the necessary land. Webster and his fellow Virginians therefore enlisted as a company in the Texas army. They suffered severe casualties during their two-year enlistment: death claimed 21 men while many others were wounded. But following their March 1839 discharge, Webster and the remainder of his original party struck out for the frontier.

A few weeks later the Websters and their comrades arrived at Hornsby's Bend in Bastrop County. Webster purchased a herd of 300 cattle and organized a train of four wagons, each pulled by four yoke[4] of oxen. Twelve free men and a black slave rode with the Webster family. A cannon trailed behind one of the wagons. The cattle would not accompany the train but would be driven up a few days later by the rest of the Virginians. On June 13, 1839, the caravan rolled away from Hornsby's Bend, bound for a new home on the North San Gabriel River.

Six miles from his destination Webster spotted a large body of armed Comanche riding in the distance. Deeming themselves of insufficient strength to withstand an attack, the men turned the train around and headed back the way they had come. Most later assumed that Webster hoped to encounter his cattle herd or, failing that, return to Hornsby's Bend.

Misfortune struck when an axle on one of the wagons broke shortly after sunset. By 3 AM the axle had been repaired and the train resumed its flight toward safety. Sunrise found the party at Brushy Creek near present-day Leander.

When John Webster had seen the Comanche from afar the previous day, he had concluded that the Indians had not seen *him*. With daylight he realized his mistake. As several hundred Comanche charged, Webster and his comrades formed the wagons into a defensive square. Immediately thereafter the Indians were upon them. One imagines that the 14 men fought bravely but against impossible odds. One by one throughout the day they fell. Finally, well after dark the last defender succumbed.

Jane Webster watched in horror as the victors carved scalps from the dead men. During the looting that followed, the Comanche slit ten sacks of coffee and spilled the contents on the ground. They smashed Jane's fine china, pocketed the silver for later use in jewelry making, and took whatever provisions they could carry. One of the Comanche found John Webster's sword. After breaking it into three pieces he shared it with two of his fellows. Four-year-old Virginia recalled years later that "that awful day still haunts my memory, but I feel happy that such sorrow can never come to me again . . . I well remember how I cried . . . ."[5]

Surveyor John Harvey was among the group that discovered the bodies of the Webster party. Dozens of bullet holes, countless arrows littering the site, and broken gun stocks spoke of the vicious nature of the fight. Harvey raced back to Bastrop to raise the alarm. Edward Burleson quickly formed a posse and sped to the battleground. John Holland Jenkins, a member of this group, later wrote, "A strange, unreal sight of horror met our eyes. Only fleshless bones scattered around remained of a brave and courageous band of men."[6] Jenkins recalled finding an old crate to serve as a coffin. Only the bones of a man named Hicks could be identified with certainty; Jenkins and the others recognized his remains because of a broken leg received at the Battle of Anahuac in 1835. Burleson and his men trailed the Comanche for 10 days but gave up when they saw signs that the band had divided into three groups.

Many days of hard riding brought the victorious Comanche home to their village. Their captors stripped Jane and her two children of their clothing, providing Jane and her son with Comanche style dress but leaving young Virginia naked. The terrified prisoners next witnessed a victory celebration, including one dance during which the performers circled a central fire waving their trophies.

Each time a dancer passed by Jane, he thrust the scalp he carried toward her face. After about 10 days of celebrating, the Comanche split into smaller groups. Each Webster went with a different band.

Virginia recalled her time in captivity as harsh and cruel. She suffered from exposure, received whippings and burns as punishment, and, on one occasion, was tied to a rope and repeatedly thrown into a river before being dragged out. Another time a group of men tied her to a horse and turned it loose. They then chased excitedly after the animal until it stopped from exhaustion.

Jane received harsh treatment as well but did manage a trick upon her captors. The Comanche repeatedly asked her how to make gunpowder, evidently assuming that all Anglos were in on this secret. Tired of the constant queries, Jane finally stated that gunpowder consisted of a mixture of coals and sand. The Comanche immediately filled several pots with the two substances and added water, which they then brought to a boil. When most of the water had boiled off they dried and pulverized what was left. Obviously, this creation failed to ignite but, instead of punishing Jane, the Comanche merely assumed that white men had not shared the production formula with their women.

Periodically the individual Comanche bands would meet up, at which time Virginia enjoyed brief reunions with her mother and brother. Jane attempted escape during gatherings at Enchanted Rock and Santa Fe but was caught with her children each time. In February 1840 she tried again. The bands had reunited at Devil's Creek in what is now Gillespie County. There Jane Webster witnessed the murders of six white captives. Later she overheard that, if the upcoming prisoner exchange in San Antonio did not go well, all of the captives would be killed. She stuffed some dried buffalo tongue into a pouch, grabbed Virginia, and left the camp.

Virginia later recalled being carried by her mother throughout their arduous journey to San Antonio. When the tongue ran out they ate raw fish and whatever roots Jane could dig up. They traveled only at night and avoided trails and watering spots. About three miles outside of San Antonio Jane collapsed under a live oak tree. Half-starved and exhausted, she had all but given up when the Mexican trading party mentioned earlier came along. The train boss wrapped his coat around scantily clad Jane, another man found a blanket for Virginia, and the escapees rode into San Antonio with the caravan. Despite the disastrous council, the Comanche delivered up Virginia's brother a few days later.

Jane Webster died July 29, 1849. Virginia attributed her early death to the travails of their captivity. Virginia's brother later attended college before enlisting in the army during the U. S. War with Mexico. He died from wounds received at the Battle of Monterrey. Virginia initially went back to her home state with her mother and brother but returned to Texas with an uncle after her mother's death. In 1853 she married M. G. Strickland. The newlyweds moved to the same Williamson County land intended as the Webster family home by Virginia's father John. Mr. Strickland died in 1865 and Virginia, after outliving another husband, moved to Oregon and then California, where she spent the remainder of her life. At age 76 she wrote, "In looking back over my past life, full of sorrows and grief, I wonder how I could have endured it all and live to be as old as I am . . . Texas has many charms for me, yet I suppose nearly all whom I once knew have passed away and have ceased from troubling."[7]

VISIT THE SITES

- John Webster and his fallen comrades lie in the Davis Cemetery on Ranch Road 2243 east of

Leander. To reach the cemetery, head east for about 2 miles on RR 2243 as it leads away from old Highway 183. The cemetery, which is on the left, contains a marker over the grave site. ⑩

- There is another marker describing the attack on old Highway 183 just south of its intersection with RR 2243. It sits on the west side of the road in the company of two other unrelated historical markers. ⑪

ENDNOTES

1. The primary source for this chapter is an account written by Virginia Webster in 1913, which appeared in the November 1923 edition of *Frontier Times*. Other sources include J. W. Wilbarger, *Indian Depredations in Texas* (Austin: Eakin Press and Statehouse Press, 1985, reprint of the original 1889 edition), pp. 19-25, and John Holmes Jenkins, III, ed., *Recollections of Early Texas: The Memoirs of John Holland Jenkins* (Austin: University of Texas Press, 2003), pp. 80-84. There are several discrepancies among these three accounts, the most important being the name of Virginia's father, which she gives as John while Wilbarger calls him James. Also, Wilbarger states that the attack on the Webster party occurred in 1838; Virginia Webster gives a date of 1839.

2. *Handbook of Texas Online*, s.v. "Council House Fight," http://www.tshaonline.org/handbook/online/articles/CC/btc1.html (accessed July 27, 2009).

3. *Frontier Times*, November 1923, vol. 1, no. 2, p. 19.

4. A yoke of oxen includes two of the animals.

5. *Frontier Times*, November 1923, vol. 1, no. 2, p. 19.

6. John Holmes Jenkins, III, ed., *Recollections of Early Texas: The Memoirs of John Holland Jenkins* (Austin: University of Texas Press, 2003), p. 81.

7. *Frontier Times*, p. 20.

The stone marker describing the attack on the Webster party is located on old Highway 183 just south of Ranch Road 2243. The other two markers are unrelated.

The remains of those killed in the attack on the Webster party lie in the Davis Cemetery on Ranch Road 2243 about two miles east of old Highway 183.

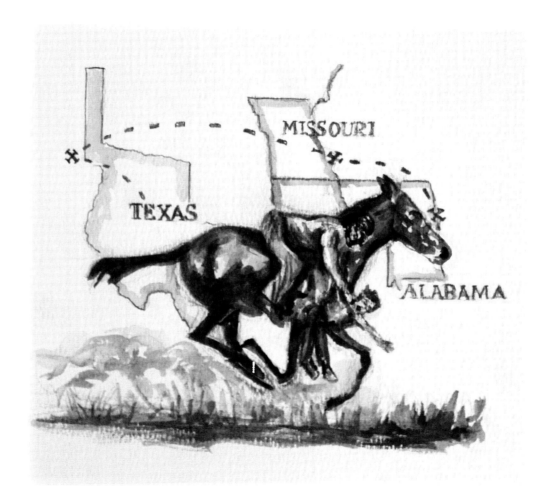

13

A BIRTHDAY TO FORGET

ON JANUARY 22, 1841, WHICH WAS his ninth birthday, Fayette Smith scrambled up onto a horse behind his father to begin what he thought would be a quick trip to fetch the family hogs. Two years would pass before his return. Fayette's father, Judge James Witherspoon Smith, never came back.

Tennessean James Smith married Angelina Stamps in Alabama around 1830. By 1834 the couple had three children, including Fayette, older daughter Caroline, and Lorena, the youngest. Smith attended the first public sale of Austin property on August 1, 1839, at which he purchased a lot on the north side of West Pecan Street between San Antonio and Guadalupe streets.[1] Shortly thereafter, he moved his family to the new seat of Texas government.

Although in 1841 the Smith house sat three blocks within the western limit of Austin, beyond lay only the "beaten track of the Indians into town from the pass of Mount Bonnell." This path, the westward continuation of Pecan Street, "secluded as it was, became their main inlet to the town. It was a sheltered road, never traveled at night by whites, so the Indians claimed right of way, and all full moons brought moccasin tracks in abundance."[2] It was along this potentially dangerous road that James Smith and his son set out after their hogs.

Disaster struck the Smiths about a half mile beyond Shoal Creek[3] in the form of five Comanche suddenly springing from the brush. Young Fayette heard rifle fire, but it was a Comanche arrow that shattered James Smith's left arm, glanced upward, and struck Fayette on the forehead. Smith's startled horse wheeled uncontrollably before dashing away from the attackers. The two riders might have escaped but for an unlucky break; as their frightened mount raced under a tree, a low hanging branch swept Fayette and his father from the saddle. One of the Indians immediately killed James. Another scooped up young Fayette before escaping with the raiding party to the northwest.

Within a month Fayette Smith and his captors fell in with the main body of the Comanche. The tribe continued heading northwest for another two or three months before encountering a party of Mexican traders, to whom Fayette was sold. Upon reaching Taos, New Mexico, the traders turned the boy over to an American named John Rowland. A hopeful Fayette gave Rowland his mother's name and address but, even if the American had wanted to send a letter, there was no mail service between Taos and the Republic of Texas. In fact, Mexico and Texas were still technically at war.

Meanwhile, Fayette's uncle William Smith had set out from Austin in pursuit of his nephew. Failing to find the boy in Santa Fe, where he had assumed a captive would be taken, he continued along the major trading route between Mexico and the United States and wound up in St. Louis. Rowland evidently had the same idea. He sent Fayette with an overland train along the same route, but the train's destination was Independence rather than St. Louis. There a man named Lewis Jones took charge of the boy and successfully contacted Smith's maternal grandfather in Talledega, Alabama. Grandfather Stamps collected Fayette from Jones and took him back to Alabama. The boy's mother arrived a short time thereafter. She and Fayette returned to Texas, but Mrs. Smith had experienced enough of Austin. In Fayette's absence the newly widowed woman had moved with her two daughters to the safer town of Washington, where Fayette passed the remainder of his youth.[4] And, despite having lost both his father and his freedom to the Comanche, Fayette Smith forgave them by saying, "I had no more experience with the Indians, and I do not want any more, yet I hold no ill will toward them, as I think that they have been badly treated and robbed of a country, the best for their purpose in the world."[5]

VISIT THE SITE

- James Smith purchased block 73, lot 2 at the auction of August 1, 1839. The section of this block facing the north side of West Pecan (6th) Street was divided into lots 1 through 4 from west to east. The Smith house therefore would have been adjacent to the northeast corner lot at San Antonio and West 6th streets. Frank Brown recalled that the Smiths lived a block to the west, between San Antonio and Nueces. However, he put this recollection to paper decades after the fact. Julia Lee Sinks claimed that her house on West Pecan, which was on the same block as James Smith's purchase, was the westernmost residence on West Pecan Street at that time. **⑱**

- The precise location of the attack upon James and Fayette Smith can only be estimated. If Frank Brown's statement that it was a half mile west of Shoal Creek is accurate, the attack took place along West 6th Street between Harthan Street and Winflo Drive.

ENDNOTES

1. Austin City Lots, Texas State Archives.

2. Julia Lee Sinks, *Early Days in Texas: Reminiscences of Julia Lee Sinks,* Julia Lee Sinks vertical file, Barker Center for American History, The University of Texas at Austin.

3. Frank Brown, *Annals of Travis County and the City of Austin, Chapter VIII,* Austin History Center, Austin, Texas. Frank Brown was a boyhood friend of Fayette Smith.

4. John Henry Brown, *Indian Wars and Pioneers of Texas* (Austin: L. E. Daniell, 1880), pp. 497-498. John Henry Brown states that these details came from his interview of Fayette Smith.

5. *Ibid.,* p. 498.

Northeast view on West 6th (Pecan) Street from San Antonio Street. The Smith family lived in a house on what is now the parking lot for the four-story hotel at the far end of the block.

14

THE PIG WAR

WHAT DO PIGS, POLITICS, PRIDE, and a Frenchman named Pluyette have in common? Ordinarily, nothing. The history of the Republic of Texas is, however, anything *but* ordinary. Early players on the Texas stage had a knack for transforming unremarkable proceedings into fascinating tales of folly and misadventure. In fact, the Republic's most enduring saga, the martyrdom of the men defending the Alamo, transpired only because Texian commanders Jim Bowie and William Travis defied orders and military logic by stubbornly attempting to hold a strategically useless position against Santa Anna's vastly superior force. And Santa Anna could have achieved victory at the Alamo while denying the rebellion its greatest propaganda tool simply by besieging the stronghold until the Texians capitulated instead of ordering the attack against it. To return to the original question: while pigs, politics, pride, and a Frenchman named Pluyette should have had *nothing* in common, these four elements united in 1841 to trigger a minor feud, which in turn set off an international dispute between the infant Republic of Texas and the Kingdom of France.

Austin residents thrilled at the arrival of the new French Chargé d'Affaires, Jean Pierre Isidore Alphonse Dubois de Saligny, in their city January 1840. That the French king would send an official representative to the Texas capital bestowed a sense of legitimacy on the new town, whose frontier location seemed foolhardy to many Texas citizens.[1] Lodging options were few, but Saligny secured rooms for himself and his entourage in Richard and Mary Bullock's hotel on the northwest corner of Congress Avenue and Pecan (6th) Street. A pleased Saligny wrote, "The welcome that I received in this country . . . leaves nothing to be desired."[2]

Shortly after Saligny's arrival, most Texas lawmakers returned home when the Fourth Texas Congress adjourned in February 1840. With little to do in Austin, Saligny prepared to leave as well for a trip to Houston and New Orleans. Finding the bill he received from Richard Bullock much higher than expected, Saligny offered a lesser sum, which Bullock angrily refused. Saligny therefore left town with an unpaid debt and a new enemy.

Saligny naturally couldn't stay at Bullock's upon his return to Austin in July. He managed to find a "sort of miserable wood cabin composed of three rooms" to rent on the southeast corner of Guadalupe and West Pecan streets, for which he once again felt overcharged at 500 francs a month.[3] Needing an office as well, he procured a small building on the south side of the 100 block of East Pecan. The four-block walk between the two buildings led right past Saligny's nemesis, Richard Bullock. Finally, recognizing the need for plusher surroundings, Saligny purchased 21 acres on a hill east of town and began construction on a house more suitable for the representative of one of the most powerful nations on earth.

Count de Saligny perceived great opportunity in his position and evidently saw no wrong in personally profiting from his efforts to further the interests of his government. The cause of France conveniently coincided with his own in the form of what became known as the Franco-Texienne Bill. Saligny successfully lobbied James Mayfield, of whom he privately wrote possessed "less than mediocre capacity and . . . an extreme ignorance,"[4] to introduce this legislation into the House of Representatives January 12, 1841. The new law would grant a huge tract of frontier land to a French corporation created by Saligny and others to bring French immigrants to Texas. The corporation would build and maintain 20 forts along the frontier as protection against Indian attack. In return, Saligny and his partners would receive tax breaks, trade rights with Mexico, mineral rights, and duty-free importation of certain goods into the Republic.

Hoping to win congressional support for his scheme, Saligny transformed his West Pecan Street home into an Austin social hub. At least twice a week, beginning in November 1840, he treated senators, representatives, cabinet members, and other luminaries to extravagant dinners accompanied by fine French wine, expensive cigars, and numerous delicacies otherwise unavailable on the Texas frontier. Sam Houston and Mirabeau Lamar were frequent guests, as was anyone else in a position to further Saligny's cause. The Frenchman's efforts bore fruit in the form of an invitation to speak in the House of Representatives. He dazzled many in the chamber by producing "a most splendid map, about six feet square, representing in rainbow colors, those various tracts of country proposed to be granted . . . with twenty fortifications thereon, plotted with all the ingenuity of a polytecnic [sic] graduate . . . ."[5]

Saligny's success must have seemed inevitable when the House approved the measure January 23, 1841. The bill received an additional boost with President *pro tem* Anson Jones' public support for the bill. But disaster arrived in the person of Vice President David Burnet, temporarily serving as chief executive during President Mirabeau Lamar's absence in the United States for medical treatment. Burnet, of whom Saligny held a low opinion,[6] let it be known that he would veto the Franco-Texienne Bill. Disheartened Senate supporters threw in the towel, failing even to call for a final vote on the measure.

Enter the pigs. Richard Bullock's pigs, to be precise. Like many of his Austin neighbors, Bullock raised hogs for food. Like many others, he also neglected to confine them to his property, preferring instead to let them roam the town's empty spaces in search of something to eat. But, while individual families might own one or two roaming animals, Bullock, with his many hungry guests, possessed dozens. Inevitably, some of the hungry hogs found their way into private gardens. And just as inevitably, many of these invaded the nearby garden of the French Chargé d'Affaires, Alphonse de Saligny.

Saligny's losses to the ravenous pigs went beyond mere vegetables. Three of them one day exploited an open door to enter his bedroom, trample official papers, and eat his bed linens. On another occasion, one of Saligny's servants suffered minor injury when a group of hogs charged into the French stable to get at the horse feed. Through his servants Saligny complained repeatedly to Richard Bullock who, not surprisingly, did little if anything to stop the depredations.

Saligny's humiliating defeat in the Texas Congress transformed his annoyance at these porcine incursions into rage. When he ordered his servants to kill any animal straying onto his property, several unlucky pigs quickly succumbed. A perfect opportunity to dispose of at least some of the dead hogs then arose in the form of one of Saligny's famous dinner parties. Imagine Richard Bullock's reaction the following morning when one of the dinner guests mischievously complimented him on the delicious pork served the night before at Count de Saligny's house!

Poor Eugene Pluyette paid the price for this latest insult to Richard Bullock's pride. The Frenchman undoubtedly kept to the far side of Pecan Street as he passed Bullock's hotel February 19, 1841, while walking to Saligny's office building. Pluyette would have known of the rancor between his boss and the angry hotel owner; he may have even killed one or two of Bullock's hogs himself. With self-righteous fury, Bullock charged across the intersection upon spying Pluyette. When a verbal harangue failed to elicit a satisfactory response, Bullock attacked the Frenchman with his walking stick. Pluyette eluded the first attempt, but further blows found their mark until the battered man sprinted to the safety of the French office.

Upon learning of the incident, an outraged Saligny immediately composed a letter of protest to the Texas Secretary of State. Unfortunately for him, the one Texan whose abilities Saligny least respected, James Mayfield, had just been appointed to that post by acting President Burnet. Mayfield coyly promised to look into the matter and punish any person who had broken the law. Richard Bullock countered with a petition to Burnet complaining not only of Saligny's unpaid hotel bill but also the dead hogs that Saligny's men had destroyed "most maliciously and wantonly . . . with pitchforks and pistols . . . ."[7]

Unsatisfied with Mayfield's promised investigation, Saligny unwisely wrote another note demanding Bullock's immediate punishment. Mayfield informed Saligny that he had handed the matter over to the courts and that a hearing was scheduled for February 23. Saligny then somewhat haughtily notified Mayfield that, although he could allow Pluyette to provide a written statement of the facts, he could not insult the dignity of France by having his servant testify in a court of law. At which point Mayfield told Saligny that, since the matter was now in the hands of the judge, there was nothing else he could do.

A month-long lull did little to calm either party. On March 25 Saligny attempted to visit his American counterpart Colonel Flood in his room at Bullock's. The innkeeper stopped him at the door. Saligny claimed that Bullock shook his fist at his adversary, grabbed him by the collar, and evicted him with the threat, "the first time that you come back here, I shall beat you up."

His pride wounded almost beyond repair, Saligny foolishly fired his biggest gun. Attempting to force James Mayfield into action, he notified the Secretary of State that he was suspending operations of the French legation until he had received instructions from the French government. Recognizing a golden opportunity to rid himself of the entire affair, Mayfield replied that he was therefore compelled to revoke Saligny's diplomatic immunity. President Lamar's wish to avoid the embarrassment of seeing Saligny arrested for his unpaid hotel bill prompted him to request the recall of the French Chargé d'Affaires. A humiliated Saligny left Austin, never to return.

Construction of Saligny's house east of town had not yet been completed at the time of his departure. Having loaned the residence to fellow Frenchman Henri Castro, Saligny later complained from afar that his friend was staging dinner parties of his own at Saligny's expense. Furthermore, among Castro's guests had been "two or three individuals who for nearly a year have been continuously conspicuous for the impudence of their invectives against France and her representative."[8]

There is no proof, but it is satisfying to speculate that one of these unwanted guests was a gloating Richard Bullock. If so, his triumph proved short-lived. While staying at a Galveston hotel in June 1842, Bullock ran into James Mayfield, the man who had frustrated Alphonse Saligny's efforts to have Bullock punished for attacking Eugene Pluyette. Bullock demanded payment of a $600 hotel bill owed by Mayfield. An astonished Mayfield argued that his support of Bullock the previous year rendered such a demand inappropriate. A fistfight ensued, after which Bullock attempted to claim Mayfield's horse and carriage as partial payment, only to discover that Mayfield's Galveston landlord had already done so. An enraged Bullock threatened a lawsuit and stormed off. On his way back to Austin, he contracted "brain fever" and died.

VISIT THE SITES

- Saligny's house, now known as the French Legation Museum and operated by the Daughters of the Republic of Texas, still stands on the hill overlooking Austin at 802 San Marcos Street. There is a small parking lot for visitors at the corner of Embassy and East 9th streets. Guided tours of the house and grounds are available. **㉕**

- Bullock's hotel stood on the northwest corner of West 6th (Pecan) Street and Congress Avenue. **❾**

- Bullock accosted Eugene Pluyette in the neighborhood of his hotel, after which the Frenchman fled to Saligny's office building on the south side of the 100 block of East 6th just before Brazos Street. **㉖**

- The house and garden so irresistible to Bullock's hogs was on the southeast corner lot at West 6th and Guadalupe streets. **⓫**

ENDNOTES

1. For example, Brazoria County Senator and later President Anson Jones wrote in his diary, "No policy could possibly have been more unwise than the removal of the seat of government to Austin . . . ." Anson Jones, *Memoranda and Official Correspondence Relating to the Republic of Texas, its History and Annexation* (Chicago: The Rio Grande Press, Inc., 1966), p. 34.

2. Saligny to M. le Marechal, January 30, 1840. Katherine Hart, ed., *Alphonse in Austin* (Austin: The Encino Press, 1967), p. 14.

3. *Ibid.,* p. 31.

4. Hart, p. 44.

5. *Texas Centinel,* July 1, 1841.

6. Of Burnet, Saligny wrote, "Sick as he is, I still prefer General Lamar as President over Judge Burnet. The inflexible and brittle character of the Vice-President, his pedantry and vanity, his smallness and pettiness of mind, his utter lack of candor-not to mention his secret antipathy for France concealed by pleasant and intimate relations that have so far existed between the Legation of the King and the government." Nancy Nichols Barker, ed., *The French Legation in Texas* (Austin: Texas Historical Association, 1971), p. 176.

7. Hart, p. 49.

8. From a letter by Saligny written April 11, 1842, as quoted in Nancy Nichols Barker, ed., *The French Legation in Texas* (Austin: Texas Historical Association, 1971), p. 301.

Alphonse de Saligny's house and garden sat here on the southwest corner of Guadalupe and West 6th (Pecan) streets.

View from the northwest corner of Congress Avenue and 6th (Pecan) Street, site of Richard Bullock's hotel. Bullock attacked Eugene Pluyette somewhere in this vicinity, after which Pluyette fled to Saligny's office in the 100 block of East 6th.

House built for Alphonse de Saligny. Saligny never lived in the completed building, which is now a museum at 802 San Marcos Street.

15

ANSON JONES' SLEEPLESS NIGHT

THOSE OPPOSING AUSTIN AS THE SEAT of government in its earliest days often cited danger of Indian attack as reason enough for a more eastern location. After providing details of a Comanche raid on Austin, the editor of the *San Augustine Journal and Advertiser* concluded by asking, "What, say you now gentle Congressman, to the safety of the present location of the seat of government; *we rather guess* you had better move your head quarters, or the Comanches will find permanent locations of your *head* rights and no mistake; for at their second coming, they may happen to want wigs, and make your scalps supply the demand."[1] Frontier residents ridiculed such sentiments, but their legitimacy was clear to early Austininte William Walsh, who recalled, "It would take too much space . . . to give a complete list of those killed by the Indians in the first ten years of the city's life."[2]

Although Massachusetts native Anson Jones agreed with Austin's critics, he nevertheless acquiesced once the government had taken up residence there.[3] Like many of his fellow Texas citizens, Jones had found nothing but failure in the United States. When the medical degree he earned from Philadelphia's Jefferson Medical College wasn't enough to lift him from poverty, he left that city for New Orleans. Disappointment followed him, and in 1833 he heeded a friend's advice by emigrating to Texas, where he opened a medical practice in Brazoria. After a stint with the Texian army that placed him at the Battle of San Jacinto, Jones returned to Brazoria to resume his medical practice but soon also increasingly involved himself in politics. By the fall of 1839, he had gained a senate seat in the Fourth Texas Congress, the first to convene in the new capitol in Austin.

Lodging was scarce in earliest Austin. By the time of Jones' arrival, the few hotels had filled to capacity, but the Brazoria senator was able to secure a room in the home of acquaintance Edwin Waller. President Mirabeau Lamar had selected Waller as the agent in charge of constructing Austin. Given the enormity of his challenge, Waller likely spent little time in his house at the intersection of Mulberry (10th) Street and Congress Avenue. He therefore may or may not have been present during the most memorable night Jones spent as a guest in Waller's home.

Senator Jones experienced no difficulty falling asleep on the evening of March 12, 1840. About 10 o'clock, however, he awoke to the cry of "Indians!" Tortured screams in the darkness convinced him that this was no false alarm. One can well imagine that sleep eluded him throughout the remainder of the night.

Many of Austin's citizens responded to the alarm by grabbing a weapon and searching the dark city streets. They came across the lifeless body of James Headley, with its throat cut, scalp removed, and chest pierced by multiple bullet holes. Meanwhile, the attackers had rounded up most of the town's horses and driven them off. Frustrated Austinites stood anxious guard throughout the city until dawn.

Shortly after sunrise came a report of a large body of Indians assembled on the Colorado River a few miles to the southeast. While racing to this spot, town residents encountered the body of another victim, a butcher named William Ward. They counted 10 arrows protruding from the corpse; blood also oozed from two bullet wounds. Finding no Indians at the river, the posse returned to Austin. Edward Burleson then returned from the countryside to report finding a deserted Indian campground four miles to the north. A large group of mounted men followed him back to the site but were unable to track down the city's attackers.

This daring raid shook any remaining complacency about the frontier's dangers from the minds of the people of Austin. Cries for revenge arose not only from Austinites, but from Anglo-Texans everywhere. The editor of Houston's *The Morning Star* blustered, "Such a daring outrage has highly exasperated the feelings of the citizens of Austin, and they seem resolved to exterminate the bloody and thieving rascals--they will shoot them down whenever and wherever they are met."[4] Anson Jones's subsequent diary entries tell of "constant" Indian alarms, militia call-ups, fortifications in the city, and intermittent panic. Despite his ridicule[5] of some of these measures, his entry of June 12, 1840, notes, "Stood guard over the town all night."[6]

Given his experience in Austin, Anson Jones could not have been disappointed when Mirabeau Lamar's presidential successor Sam Houston pulled the government out of the city after a series of Mexican incursions in 1842. But Houston's own successor as chief executive was none other than

Anson Jones. It was President Jones who oversaw transfer of the government back to Austin in 1845. Although Austinites undoubtedly still harbored concerns about Indian attack, a letter to Jones from Joseph Daniels suggests that such fears were subsiding: "Our city [Austin] is very lively at this time, being the New Year's Eve. We have a cotillion party, and a deputation of Major Western's pets from the Ton-ke-wahs are here, most gloriously drunk. The United States troop of dragoons paraded our streets to-day in full dress."[7]

Thereafter, any sleepless nights endured by Anson Jones in Austin resulted from political squabbles or indigestion, not Indian attack.

VISIT THE SITE

- Edwin Waller's house sat on the southwest corner of the intersection of Congress Avenue and Mulberry (10th) Street. **㉔**

- The precise locations of the killings of James Headley and William Ward are unknown.

ENDNOTES

1. *San Augusting Journal and Adverstiser,* as quoted in the *Austin City Gazette,* December 16, 1840. This particular attack, in which a party of mounted Comanche supposedly rode screaming through the city in the middle of the day, never took place.

2. *Austin Statesman,* February 3, 1924.

3. Jones wrote in his diary, "No policy could possibly have been more unwise than the removal of the seat of Govt to Austin, and corrupt means were used to place it there. But now that so much money has been expended

I shall be for its remaining at that place." Anson Jones, *Memoranda and Official Correspondence Relating to the Republic of Texas, its History and Annexation* (Chicago: The Rio Grande Press Inc., 1966), p. 34.

4. *The Morning Star,* March 21, 1840.

5. For example, on June 7, 1840, Jones wrote, "The fool order calling out the *militia,* came out yesterday." Jones, p. 38.

6. *Ibid.*

7. *Ibid.,* p. 508.

Southwest corner of the intersection of Congress Avenue and 10th (Mulberry) Street, site of Edwin Waller's house in 1840.

16

DANGER IN THE NIGHT[1]

THE TWO YOUNG LADIES IGNORED the frequent false notes bouncing from the guitar played by one of them as they sang,

Thou, thou, e'en as I love thee
Say, say, wilt thou love me?
Thoughts, thoughts, tender and true, love,
Say wilt thou cherish for me?

Stars lighting the night sky provided a false sense of security. The girls sat on the front steps of a small house, the uppermost residence on the west side of Congress Avenue in 1841. One of them held a small baby. Absorbed in romantic reverie, they began the final verse,

Yes, yes, yes, yes,
Say wilt thou . . . INJUNS! INJUNS!

The last words echoed not with the soft feminine voices of Julia Lee Sinks and her companion Martha Clemens but with the dissonant, masculine cry of a terrified man. It came from afar but carried closer with each repetition. Julia and her friend jumped up. After a moment's hesitation, they dashed inside the house to search for the percussion caps and pistols that would be their protection. When Julia's efforts proved fruitless, she took the baby so that Martha could look. To her surprise, Julia noticed that her fear evaporated as she cooed soothing words to the infant in her arms. With the pistols located, she started to hand the baby back to its mother when the man raising the ruckus burst into the room.

Nothing in his native Switzerland had prepared John Wahrenberger[2] to expect that a trip to the mill could cost him his life. But on his way back to the house of his employer Louis Cooke[3] with the meal, Wahrenberger had been attacked by an unknown number of Indians. He stood before the two startled women with the meal sack still slung over his back. That the sack had saved his life seemed clear from the multiple arrows protruding from it, none of which had penetrated far enough to injure Wahrenberger. But another had sliced through his arm and into the front of his coat, "holding him like a duck skewed for roasting." Finding herself surprisingly amused in the face of this horror, Julia had to suppress a laugh.

Wahrenberger continued his cries for assistance and, when none came, let loose with a string of oaths "that seemed like a flaming sword to guard the entrance, imprecations at the Indians, at the peoples [sic] for not coming to the rescue." The embarrassed women coaxed the wounded man to lie down on the floor. Placing part of the meal sack under Wahrenberger's head for a pillow, Julia extricated the arrow by pulling it the rest of the way through the injured arm. By the time she had finished bandaging him, "John was himself again."

At last help arrived and the house filled with people, many of them armed. Outside, town residents ran haphazardly through the streets in search of the attackers. One witness later reported that "the men ran through town like a gang of wild mustangs . . . reason had completely forsaken them." When a man named Clendennin failed to respond quickly enough to a challenge from Captain Nicholson, the captain shot him. Luckily, the wound was not severe.[4]

Julia's brother arrived to escort her back to their house on West Pecan (6th) Street. On the way they encountered a company of soldiers led by Felix Huston. The contrast between the rhythmic, noisy marching of the soldiers and the stealthy tactics of the Indians struck Julia as slightly ridiculous because the more regimented Anglo approach seemed out of place on the Texas frontier. Nevertheless, she interpreted the attackers' hit-and-run tactic as proof that "the Indians are great cowards . . . ."

Once he calmed down, John Wahrenberger told his listeners that he had met the Indians after heading east at the foot of Capitol Hill. Immediately turning to retrace his steps back toward Louis Cooke's house, he had raised the cry that interrupted Julia and Martha's singing. As Wahrenberger raced into the house, Cooke dashed outside with loaded pistols and fired. After so narrowly escaping death, John Wahrenberger exclaimed, "Oh! Mine Got! What a Texas dis is! I tink I go back to Sweetzerland!"[5] At daylight, residents found several arrows sticking in the front of the house as well as in a nearby post oak tree. They also discovered that Louis Cooke's aim had been accurate. Not far from the house a pool of blood darkened the ground, while a trail of bloodstains led past the house toward the west.[6]

Julia Lee Sinks lived in Austin at a time when such incidents did not always end well for city residents. Standing out among her memories of life in the young capital was the "dead house" on Congress Avenue, where the bodies of those killed by Indians were kept before burial. Years later, as she wrote down the story of John Wahrenberger and his comical appearance in the doorway of Louis Cooke's house, she recalled the mixed emotions of the frontier by observing, "merriment stands just on the confines of sorrow."

VISIT THE SITES

- Louis Cooke's house stood on the northwest corner of Congress Avenue and Mulberry (10th) Street. ⓬

- Leaving Cooke's house to go to the mill, John Wahrenberger walked north along Congress until turning east to follow a path that, according to Julia Lee Sinks, "crossed the flat in front of the capitol." ❸

- The wounded Indian fled westward past the current site of the Governor's Mansion (the grounds of which are bounded by Colorado, Lavaca, 10th, and 11th streets). ⓭

ENDNOTES

1. Unless otherwise noted, details presented in this chapter are from Julia Lee Sinks, comp. Frances Brady Underwood, *Early Days in Texas* (Austin: Nortex Press, 2005), pp. 57-59.

2. Swiss-born Wahrenberger arrived in New Orleans in 1836 and moved to Austin in 1839. He eventually became quite prosperous in the city as a baker, café and hotel owner, and real estate investor. He died in 1864. *Handbook of Texas Online*, s.v. "Wahrenberger, John," http://www.tshaonline.org/handbook/online/articles/WW/fwa10.html (accessed April 15, 2010).

3. Cooke, one of the five government commissioners selecting the site for the city of Austin, hired Wahrenberger as a gardener.

4. Jake Snively to James H. Starr, February 23, 1841. Austin File Chronological, 1841, sec. 5, Austin History Center, Austin, Texas.

5. J. W. Wilbarger, *Indian Depredations in Texas* (Austin: Eakin Press and Statehouse Press, 1985), p. 271.

6. This trail of blood followed a path that led past the site of the current Governor's Mansion.

Louis Cooke's house stood here on the northwest corner of the intersection of Congress Avenue and 10th (Mulberry) Street.

The hill on which the capitol now sits was undeveloped at the time of the attack on John Wahrenberger. After leaving Louis Cooke's house, Wahrenberger walked north to this hill before turning east, shortly after which he encountered his assailants.

17

FOX KILLED IN THE CORN

AUSTIN IN THE DAYS OF THE REPUBLIC was primarily a city of men. The few women in the settlement tended to band together at any opportunity, each mother "[taking] her family of cubs with her"[1] to find companionship in the home of that day's hostess. Women enjoyed trading information and performing chores together; children looked forward to the opportunity of a day spent among peers.

One warm February day in 1842, six-year-old William Walsh tagged along with his mother to the Wooldridge home, a large house on the west side of Congress Avenue below Pecan Street. After a noon meal prepared by Ann Wooldridge, the women shooed their youngsters outside to play in the fenced back yard while they continued their visiting indoors. A suggestion from one of the boys for a swimming expedition to Shoal Creek received an enthusiastic response; soon the entire pack of boys began tearing westward through the strip of post oak forest which followed the Colorado River.[2] Within moments of reaching the creek, the boys had stripped off their clothes and plunged into the chilly water.

Those unfamiliar with Austin winters might think it unusual for a February day to be warm enough for swimming. In fact, such days are common. Only 24 hours before Williams Walsh's creek expedition, Julia Lee Sinks had accompanied her sister, a friend named Mrs. Coombs, and Mrs. Coombs' young son on a pleasant walk leading southward from the Coombs house along the eastern bank of Shoal Creek to the "Cliff Cottage." Once the home of an elderly man and his son, the crude structure now stood vacant above the creek, its outdoor table and overgrown arbor still providing fruit, shade, and peaceful seclusion to the occasional visitor. The previous occupants had tended a field of fine watermelons on the creek's western bank, and although the house remained empty the field had been claimed by an Irishman man named Fox. Upon arriving at the deserted house, Mrs. Sinks and her companions shuddered slightly at the thought of their exposed position. They therefore breathed a sigh of relief to see Fox and his black slave working in the nearby field.[3]

The next morning Mrs. Sinks noticed Fox driving his oxcart of garden tools past the Sinks house on West Pecan Street. The sight of Fox reminded her of how foolish the previous day's trek had been. She had lain awake much of the night after her safe return pondering the terrible price she might have paid had the party been spotted by Indians.

Every Anglo mother on the Texas frontier stressed to her children the threat of Indian attack. William Walsh and his friends would not have ventured to Shoal Creek had they perceived danger. They knew of the field on the west bank above the creek. They also knew that Mr. Fox and his slave would be at work plowing the field for corn while they played in the water. The sudden cry of terror from above therefore caught the boys by surprise.

One of the boys sprang from the water and bounded up the east bank. Looking back across the creek, he saw several Indians gathered around the defenseless Fox, by now writhing in agony from the arrows and spears piercing his body. As the attackers scalped the dying man, William Walsh and his comrades raced up the east bank and fled toward the safety of town.

Sprinting through the grass, Walsh heard the beat of the Indian alarm drum in the distance. The women in Mrs. Wooldridge's house heard it too. As one they rose and dashed outside, shrieking in horror at the discovery of their children's absence. But suddenly the tall grass began disgorging naked boys. As he entered the yard, each boy was grabbed by his mother and smothered with kisses. Walsh wrote,

> I don't know, but I am inclined to think that our naked bodies were temptations too strong to be resisted, for, in a short time, each mother, with tear-stained cheeks, was spanking her darling boy.
> Never having been a mother this proceeding is still a mystery to me.[4]

At about the same time that William Walsh received his spanking, Julia Lee Sinks was startled by the sudden appearance at her door of a breathless black man. He gasped the news of the nearby Indian raiders, and within a short time a rescue expedition headed toward Shoal Creek. Mrs. Sinks soon saw Fox's oxcart again, this time burdened with the man's body. His lifeless feet poked out from the blanket covering the corpse.[5]

Whereas William Walsh at the end of his life recalled a half-dozen attacking Indians, Thomas William Ward, in a letter to Sam Houston written within days of the incident, reported three.[6] The

Austin City Gazette claimed only two.[7] All agreed, however, that the young slave with Fox had escaped. Ward told Houston that Fox had been "shot through the breast, cut in the abdomen with a knife, and scalped." Ward's next observation startles with its tacitly implied acceptance of the dangers of frontier life. He writes, "Austin is very dull at present . . . ."

By the time of William Walsh's published recollections, Fox's cornfield had become part of the Cotton Compress. The compress disappeared years ago; a parking lot now commands the creek's western embankment. An antiquated railroad bridge still spans Shoal Creek at the site of William Walsh's 1842 swimming expedition, but the tracks on either side are long gone. No one swims in Shoal Creek any longer. The once year-round waterway now flows only in the spring or after a heavy rain. On a nice day hundreds of people walk, jog, or bike along the creek ignorant of the dramatic events that occurred within yards of their exercise path.

VISIT THE SITE

- William Walsh gives the location of his swimming hole as the point on Shoal Creek "now crossed by the International Railroad." The tracks formerly followed Third Street west from Congress Avenue; the bridge still crosses Shoal Creek between Neches Street and West Avenue. Third Street dead-ends just west of Neches and resumes two blocks west at West Avenue. Therefore, the visitor should park on the street near one of these intersections and walk the short distance to the creek. One could also approach the bridge on foot from north or south by using the Shoal Creek Hike and Bike Trail that runs between Lady Bird Lake and 38th Street. ❿

- Julia Lee Sinks and her companions began their excursion from the Coombs house on the south side of College Avenue (12th Street) between Guadalupe and San Antonio streets.[8] Walking first to Shoal Creek, they descended into the creek bed before following it south as far as the Cliff Cottage and Fox's cornfield. Her account does not specify on which side of the creek the cottage sat. ⓫

ENDNOTES

1. *The Austin Statesman,* February 3, 1924. Shortly before his death in 1924, 88-year-old William Walsh penned a series of articles about life in early Austin which appeared in 14 weekly installments of the *Austin Statesman.* This anecdote appeared in the second and third installments. Walsh and his family had moved to Austin in 1840.

2. *Ibid.* Walsh writes that the area between the river and Cedar (4th) Street contained primarily walnut, pecan, elm, and hackberry trees. Post oak dominated between Cedar and Pecan (6th). Beyond that, blackjack grew in abundance as far as Walnut (14th) Street, after which a rolling prairie dotted with clusters of live oak spread northward. Tall grass grew beneath the trees closest to the river. Above Pecan Street a blanket of wildflowers imbued the region with a patchwork of brilliant color.

3. Julia Lee Sinks, *Early Days in Texas,* comp. Frances Brady Underwood (Austin: Nortex Press, 2005), pp. 23-24.

4. *Austin Statesman,* February 10, 1924.

5. Sinks, p. 24.

6. Thomas William Ward to Sam Houston, February 23, 1842, Madge Hearn Collection, Barker Center for American History, The University of Texas at Austin.

7. *Austin City Gazette,* March 2, 1842.

8. Sinks states that the Coombs house "stood on the northwest verge of the ridge of high ground that overlooks the flat north of the capitol." At the first public sale of Austin city lots, Alfred Coombs purchased lot 7 in block 133, which was bounded by College Avenue and Guadalupe, Mesquite (11th), and San Antonio streets. Lots 5-8 span the block from east to west on the north side defined by College. Sinks, p. 24, and Austin and Galveston City Lots, Texas State Archives.

Looking northwest from a pedestrian bridge next to the railroad bridge mentioned by William Walsh. Indians killed Fox in the area now covered by a parking lot while Walsh and his friends played in Shoal Creek to the right.

Looking east along 12th Street (College Avenue) from San Antonio Street. The Coombs house sat on the south side of 12th, which is at right in the photograph.

18

PLAYING INDIAN

IN 1842, SIX-YEAR-OLD WILLIAM WALSH discovered to his great surprise that Indian children, or "papooses"[1] as he called them, "were human" too. Shortly after a devastating attack by the Comanche and Lipan Apache on the Tonkawa, about 250 Tonkawa survivors sought shelter in the city of Austin. The militarily weak Tonkawa had already thrown in their lot with the Anglo settlers, deeming these usurpers less of a threat than their indigenous enemies. Austin residents accepted the Tonkawa encampment in an oak grove on West Cedar (4th) Street as a buffer against Comanche incursions from the west. In exchange for permission to reside within the city limits, the refugees agreed to serve as sentries on Austin's most exposed flank and to participate in punitive expeditions against hostile natives. They were also invited to trade meat, wild fruit, and nuts for needed goods.

William Walsh, who lived with his family in a house on Pine (5th) Street,[2] soon overcame his preconceived notions of Indians and befriended several Tonkawa boys. One day a group of these boys appeared at the Walsh house and offered to trade a bow and arrows for a sack of sweet potatoes. After quickly agreeing to the swap, Walsh ran off with the boys to play at the Tonkawa camp. Soon they cavorted in a deep and muddy ditch, at the bottom of which "was the reddest clay I ever saw." Someone suggested using the clay to make an Indian of William. William liked the idea enough that he stripped off his clothes and allowed his playmates to smear him over completely. He tied some turkey feathers around his head and, with his bow and arrows, the transformation was complete.

Waving scraps of buffalo hide around as stand-in Comanche scalps, the boys began dancing and singing loudly. After a particularly frenzied scream, William threw back his head and, to his horror, saw his father Dennis watching from the top of the ditch. "Your mother wants you," the elder Walsh ominously intoned. He began gathering up his son's clothes. William stood transfixed, but when his father walked away the boy rediscovered his ability to move and meekly followed.

William's fear and embarrassment during the walk home evoked tears. When he and his father encountered two neighbors,[3] the elder Walsh explained that he had "just captured a little Indian and am taking him home to see if my wife can tame him." Mrs. Walsh greeted her muddied son with a perplexing silence, broken only when her husband remarked, "I think a thorough course of soap and water will remove clay and sins alike." Toward the end of his long life, William recalled the ensuing cleansing as "torture," and claimed that, "I never again had any ambition to be an Indian."

A week later, William narrowly missed another Indian adventure that ended less humorously. His mother had just made the boy his first pair of long pants, which William proudly donned before running outside so that "an astonished world might see me." Two well-known and well-liked young men, George Dolson and John Black, rode by on their way to Barton Springs and, after admiring the youngster's new pants, invited him along. Dolson called out to inform William's mother of their plans, but Mrs. Walsh expressed concern for the safety of the new pants and kept the boy at home. William trudged inside the house "with closed mouth and swelling throat" to sulk in his bed.

Two hours later the booming sound of the drum used to warn of Indian attack startled William from his self-pity. As town residents gathered in the streets to assess the threat, two saddled but riderless horses galloped into view. Horrified onlookers recoiled at the sight of the bloody saddles. Arrows protruded from the terrified animals. These were the mounts of Black and Dolson, but where were the two men?

Minutes later a search party found the scalped and mutilated bodies of Dolson and Black lying along the trail on the far side of the Colorado River. Their killers had fired from the dense brush above the trail, meaning that the two victims presented easy targets no farther away than 20 or 30 feet. More than 80 years later William Walsh recalled this day, one in which he had narrowly escaped death or captivity, as the saddest of *all* his days in Austin.

VISIT THE SITES

- According to William Walsh, the Tonkawa camped in a live oak grove along West Cedar (4th) Street near "the Walker Properties." The 1922 Austin City Directory lists Walker Properties headquarters at 310 San Antonio Street and the Walker Properties plant at 500-502 West 3rd.[4] The Tonkawa camp therefore extended along the 500 block of West Cedar (4th). **16**

- The Walsh family lived in a house on Pine (5th) Street, but William does not provide an address. It seems to me that Tonkawa boys would have been more likely to strike up friendships with boys living closest to their camp, which would imply that William lived on the west side of town. Most of the houses built in 1839, the year in which Dennis Walsh constructed his, lay within three or four blocks of Congress Avenue. The Walsh family therefore probably lived in a home on West Pine (5th) Street between the Tonkawa camp and Congress Avenue.

- William Walsh recalled that Black and Dolson died on the trail to Barton Springs as it wound around the base of the hill "just above the bridge."[5] In 1842 the undammed Colorado River flowed at the bottom of a deep channel lined with steep embankments. Therefore, the hill referred to by Walsh was probably the south embankment. The easiest place to cross the river was at the mouth of Shoal Creek, an area just south of the probable Walsh home site. It seems plausible that the two doomed men rode past the Walsh home on their way to this river crossing. While returning from the springs they were killed on a trail now covered by Lady Bird Lake that paralleled the modern walking path along Auditorium Shores. 🅐

ENDNOTES

1. In 1924 *The Austin Statesman* published a series of articles written by 88-year-old William Walsh about life in early Austin. This chapter is based upon the thirteenth installment, which appeared in the March 30 edition.

2. I have been unable to ascertain the precise location.

3. Joseph Lee and J. W. Robertson.

4. The plant produced Austex Chili, which resulted in what is now Republic Square being called "Chili Square."

5. When Walsh wrote this in 1924, the only bridge for automobiles and pedestrians in Austin crossing the Colorado River was the Congress Avenue Bridge.

500 block of West 4th (Cedar) Street, site of the 1842 Tonkawa camp.

View east on West 5th (Pine) Street from San Antonio Street. The Walsh family likely lived on this street between here and Congress Avenue.

View of the south bank of Lady Bird Lake across from the mouth of Shoal Creek. Dolsen and Black were killed near the river on a trail that is probably now under water.

Grave marker of Dolsen and Black in Oakwood Cemetery at 1601 Navasota Street.

19

GIDEON WHITE'S FATAL MISTAKE

ALABAMAN GIDEON WHITE BID HIS family farewell one winter day in 1837 and struck out for Texas. Liking what he found there, he returned to Alabama, collected his wife and children, and journeyed back to the Lone Star Republic to settle in Bastrop County. Two years later the White clan moved again, this time to a double log cabin across Shoal Creek from the bubbling waters of what came to be called Seiders Springs. White had no immediate neighbors, although the burgeoning new town of Austin lay only a few miles to the south.[1]

Gideon White plowed the land atop the creek embankment and planted crops. He met Edward Seiders, one of the first merchants in Austin, whom he hired to help manage the farm. White was soon a familiar figure in Austin as he began supplying town merchants with various types of produce and other farm goods. He became friends with Judge Joseph Lee, J. W. Wilbarger, and others. Those who had been longer on the frontier frequently warned White, as they warned all newcomers, of the danger of traveling the countryside on foot. A man caught by Indians on the prairie without the means of a speedy getaway stood little chance of survival.

In the fall of 1842,[2] there had been few recent Indian sightings in the Austin area. Gideon White thought little enough of the risk that, on the morning of October 25, he climbed the small rise behind his cabin and set off walking to find a team of oxen that he had let loose the previous night to graze. But lost cattle became a forgotten concern when White realized he had been spotted by a party of mounted Indians. The Indians wheeled their horses to give chase. Had White also been mounted, he might have escaped. Without a horse, flight only delayed the inevitable.

White sprinted toward the relative safety of his cabin by the creek but, as his attackers quickly gained ground, realized he wouldn't make it.[3] Darting behind one of the massive live oak trees clustered near his house, he turned to face his pursuers. A vicious battle ensued, in which the trapped man fired repeatedly from the cover of the oak while the Indians poured a steady stream of lead and arrows in his direction. That White's defense was not without effect was proven at the discovery, yards from his corpse, of a bloody patch of grass marking the spot where one of his assailants had fallen.[4] The many arrows and bullets embedded in the oak tree testified to White's tenacity, as well as to the Indians' persistence. Decades after the fight curiosity seekers still marveled at the battle scars displayed by this ancient tree.

After the death of Gideon White, Edward Seiders took a liking to White's daughter Louisa and married her. In 1871, after all threat of Indian attack had passed, Seiders exploited the springs that now bear his name by building a bath house on the creek, carving bathing pools in the limestone along the banks, and inviting city dwellers up for a day of leisure in the country. This business eventually petered out, and by the 1890s the bath house sat in ruins. A real estate developer acquired the property and announced plans for the Glen Ridge subdivision,[5] which would occupy the land on either side of the creek in the vicinity of the springs. As a first step, a downstream dam was built to form Alamo Lake, but a devastating 1900 flood destroyed the dam and thwarted further development. Today Seiders Oaks, as the oak grove marking the site of Gideon White's cabin is known, provides a shady rest stop along the Shoal Creek Hike and Bike Trail.

VISIT THE SITE

- Easy access to Seiders Oaks is available from the Seton Shoal Creek Hospital parking lot at 3501 Mills Avenue on the west side of Shoal Creek. Simply descend the embankment to reach the creek side footpath, turn right, and walk a few dozen yards to reach the cluster of oaks that sheltered Gideon White. There is a historical marker at the site. A concrete path leads across the creek to the still trickling springs. ⑫

- Gideon White is buried in Oakwood Cemetery at 1601 Navasota Street.

ENDNOTES

1. J. W. Wilbarger, *Indian Depredations in Texas* (Austin: Eakin Press, 1985), pp. 275-276.

2. Frank Brown, *Annals of Travis County and the City of Austin,* chap. 9, Austin History Center, Austin, Texas. J. W. Wilbarger states that White's death occurred in the spring of 1842. Brown provides the specific October date. I have found numerous incorrect dates in Wilbarger's book and am therefore inclined to go with Brown's date.

3. According to Wilbarger, White's body was found within sight of and within a quarter mile of his house.

4. Wilbarger claims that this provided proof that Wilbarger had killed one of the Indians. However, no body was found.

5. State Street, now 34th Street, formed the southern boundary of the proposed Glen Ridge, which would have extended northward to modern 38th Street. A drawing of Glen Ridge subdivision may be viewed at the Austin History Center. It shows tree-lined streets, a streetcar track along State Street, and an artificial peninsula in Alamo Lake with gazebo and manicured park.

A bicycle rider coasts along the recreational trail past the site of Gideon White's violent death.

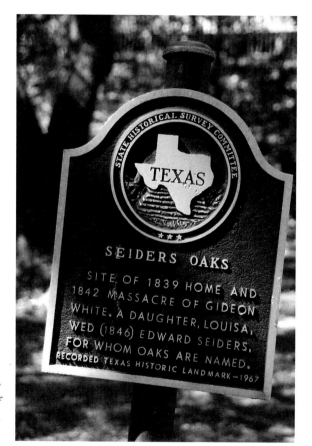

Historical marker at Seiders Oaks on Shoal Creek, site of Gideon White's frontier cabin and fatal Indian encounter.

*Gideon White's
headstone in Oakwood
Cemetery.*

20

STEALING BACK THE ARCHIVES

SAM HOUSTON'S DRUBBING OF DAVID BURNET in the 1841 presidential election caused many Austin residents to fear for their city's future.[1] Outgoing President Mirabeau Lamar had achieved a great political victory with the 1839 founding of Austin as the nation's capital on its western frontier. The soon to be ex-president's triumph came against Sam Houston's fierce opposition. Although Houston denied the intention, detractors assumed he would use his presidential power to remove the government back east. One feisty westerner dared him to try:

> We did heare that you was goin to move the seat of government . . . you swore you would do it, and then when you come to Austin and found out the boys would not let you do it you sed you never was goin to move it . . . the truth is that you are afeard . . . . Now old fellow if you want to try Ned Burlesons spunk jist try to move these papers . . . .[2]

Houston objected to locating the government seat in Austin partly out of concern for another Mexican invasion. Five years into its existence the Texas republic had still not achieved a final peace with its southern neighbor. The newly installed President warned of disaster if a Mexican army should capture Austin and the national archives. His fears seemed confirmed March 5, 1842, with the sudden appearance of General Ráfael Vásquez and several hundred Mexican soldiers in San Antonio. Just as quickly the Mexicans left, but not before Secretary of War George Hockley declared martial law in Austin and ordered the archives buried for safekeeping.

Despite the brevity of the Mexican incursion, President Houston ordered Hockley to move the archives to Washington.[3] Angry Austin residents organized under Henry Jones to resist. In addition to seizing the arsenal and Quartermaster's Department, they placed an artillery piece in a shed on the east side of Congress Avenue between Pecan (6th) and Bois d'Arc (7th) streets, from which it could be rolled and used to fire on anyone attempting to remove the archives from the Land Office two blocks north. As a further precaution, Jones also ordered the inspection of any wagon leaving Austin. President Houston hurled charges of treason at Jones, but neither Jones nor Austin residents much cared. Unwilling to risk a violent confrontation, George Hockley chose to leave the archives in Austin for the time being.

Austin citizens may have preserved their hold on the archives, but government officials obeyed the President's order to leave town. Only Land Commissioner Thomas William Ward remained to watch over his department's captive records. Tempers on both sides simmered throughout the summer. Many westerners clamored to invade Mexico; Sam Houston and his followers urged caution while continuing to insist that stubborn Austinites accede to his orders.

The Mexicans returned. On September 11, 1842, General Adrian Woll and 1500 Mexican soldiers captured San Antonio and settled in to stay. In response, a much smaller Texian force gathered along Salado Creek just outside of the occupied town, tempted Woll to attack its sheltered position, and inflicted a decisive defeat. Once again the Mexican army retreated to the Rio Grande.

By the time of General Woll's attack on San Antonio, President Houston had already attempted to convene Congress in his namesake city, which had been the capital immediately before Austin.[4] When too few legislators heeded the President's call, he issued a new directive naming Washington as the government seat. After Woll's retreat, Houston redoubled his efforts at moving the archives. He sent John Wall and Buck Pettus to Austin, but the duo made the mistake of openly loading the transport wagons before retiring to a nearby saloon for the night. Upon exiting the saloon the following morning, the two men encountered a loaded cannon aimed at them by a large crowd of angry Austin citizens. Wall tried to gut it out, but Pettus pointed to a member of the mob and said, "See here, Wall, I know that lady and she will shoot."[5] The archives stayed. Wall and Pettus left town, the latter on a horse with shaved tail, mane, and ears.

Houston persisted. He ordered Major Thomas Smith and Captain Eli Chandler to organize a force of about 20 men for the stated purpose of going on a punitive expedition against Indians. In reality, the men were to slip into Austin as quietly as possible, load up the Land Office archives, and immediately leave town. Around midday on December 30th somebody raised an Indian alarm in Austin, which quickly cleared the town of most of its fighting men, the remaining citizenry gathering for protection at Bullock's Hotel at Pecan (6th) Street and Congress Avenue. Shortly thereafter Smith, Chandler, and their armed comrades led a train of wagons west on Hickory (8th) Street to Congress before stopping in an alley behind the Land Office on the intersection's northeast corner. Physician John Robertson, having spotted the men at the Land Office, walked up the Avenue to investigate, only to be gruffly ordered away. Back at Bullock's, local innkeeper Angelina Eberly, recognizing the purpose of the intruders, urged Robertson and several other men to action by pointing across the street and shouting, "What is that cannon for?" The men rolled the piece into the street, by which time Mrs. Eberly stood ready with a lit fuse. The ensuing blast sent a round of grapeshot screaming toward the Land Office.

Startled men hurriedly loaded the last of the crates of records onto their wagons and rumbled out of town. Instead of taking the usual route eastward to Bastrop, where they might have encountered further armed and angry citizens, they headed north toward Brushy Creek. Meanwhile, the men of Austin, having heard the boom of the artillery piece, abandoned their fruitless Indian hunt and raced back to town. While they debated their next move, one of their number, a man named John Nolan,[6] attempted to impound the horse of Dr. John Marsden, who refused to yield. Nolan threatened to shoot Marsden. Captain Mark B. Lewis intervened by knocking Nolan's rifle aside, which allowed Marsden to flee the scene. Lewis' action perhaps saved Marsden but also contributed to a later encounter with Nolan that did not end as peacefully.[7]

Nightfall found Smith and the archives several miles north of Austin at Brushy Creek. They set up camp amid the ruins of an old fort.[8] Mark Lewis and a growing number of aroused locals pushed on through the darkness. By dawn they had reached and encircled Smith's force. They had also brought the artillery piece fired the day before by Angelina Eberly. Mrs. Eberly had stayed behind, but several of her fellow townsmen stood ready to blast away again should Smith fail to see the logic of their viewpoint.

Thomas Smith tried to bluff his way out of a hopeless situation. He refused an initial cry to surrender by demanding a parley with his adversaries. Two men trotted forward to talk. Smith invoked presidential authority only to be rebuffed. He continued to argue, but several of his men now spoke up, reminding their commander that they had joined him to fight Indians, not fellow Texas citizens. Seeing no other choice, the frustrated Smith yielded.

Mark Lewis immediately ordered his men to turn the wagons around and head south. A hero's welcome awaited them back in Austin. Residents cheered wildly as the archives entered town, then invited Lewis and his fellow rebels to partake of the celebratory feast they had prepared to honor the occasion. As the men ate they undoubtedly reflected upon the notion that, while Sam Houston might run the country from elsewhere, he would have to do so without the records of the General Land Office. In the minds of Austin residents, their city remained the Republic's capital.

VISIT THE SITES

- The Quartermaster's Department occupied the northeast corner of the intersection of Congress Avenue with Hickory (8th) Street. The Land Office sat immediately to the east on Hickory. Thomas Smith and Eli Chandler had placed their wagons in the space between these two structures when they were fired upon from Congress Avenue just north of Pecan (6th) Street by Angelina Eberly, Dr. Robertson, and the other Austin residents. ❷

- Mark Lewis and his fellow Austin residents recaptured the archives from Thomas Smith and Eli Chandler at the remains of Kenney's Fort on Brushy Creek. The fort itself has long since disappeared, but there is a marker and metal flag at the site. An unnamed road coursing north from a right angle turn in Sycamore Trail terminates at a water tower. A short walk east along the creek's south bank leads to the marker, which is in a large field owned by a real estate developer. The developer's website describes the location as "once a historic Fort, soon to be an exciting new Round Rock development."9 ⑮

- There is an historical marker for the fort located approximately 2.5 miles east of Interstate 35 on the south side of U.S. Highway 79 (Palm Valley Boulevard). ⑯

ENDNOTES

1. Houston won by a 3 to 1 margin. James L. Haley, *Sam Houston* (Norman: University of Oklahoma Press, 2004), p. 227.

2. John Welsh to Sam Houston, January 7, 1842, R. Niles Graham-Pease Collection, AF A8500 (1840's-1890's), Austin History Center, Austin, Texas. Edward "Ned" Burleson, a strong proponent of Austin and the West, had just won the vice presidency. By "these papers," Welsh means the national archives.

3. The town of Washington no longer exists, but the area is preserved as Washington-on-the-Brazos State Historic Site.

4. The law designating Houston as the Republic's capital stated that it would remain so until the end of the 1840 congressional session. The subsequent removal in 1839 therefore proved to be highly contentious. H. P. N. Gammel, *The Laws of Texas 1822-1897, vol. 1, First Congress* (Austin: The Gammel Book Company, 1898), p. 78.

5. *Southern Intelligencer,* March 22, 1866, as quoted in Austin File Chronological, 1842, Section 8, Austin History Center, Austin, Texas.

6. Some accounts refer to Nolan as "Noland."

7. See the chapter "Gunfight on East Pecan Street."

8. This was Kenney's Fort, built in 1839 but by 1842 abandoned and largely dismantled.

9. www.kenneysfort.com. (accessed May 3, 2009).

Northeast corner of Congress Avenue and 8th (Hickory) Street. The Quartermaster's Office occupied the corner, while the Land Office sat immediately to the east.

Sketch by Julia Robertson under the direction of her aunt, Julia Lee Sinks, a resident of Austin in 1842. The Land Office is the taller building behind the one-story Quartermaster's Department.

MORELAND HOUSE.   QUARTERMASTER'S DEPARTMENT.

This sculpture of Angelina Eberly by Patrick Oliphant is on Congress Avenue between 6th (Pecan) and 7th (Bois d'Arc) streets. The cannon was rolled into the Avenue before it was fired. The Land Office was just beyond the State Theater sign in the distance.

This marker for Kenney's Fort on U.S. Highway 79 (Palm Valley Boulevard) in Round Rock sits about a mile north of the actual fort site.

*Site of Kenney's Fort
on Brushy Creek,
where Austin residents
recaptured the national
archives. The creek flows
just behind the trees.*

21

GUNFIGHT ON EAST PECAN

WITHIN JUST A FEW YEARS OF ITS bustling 1839 start, the city of Austin gasped for survival. President Sam Houston delivered a near fatal blow in 1842 when, in response to two separate Mexican occupations of San Antonio, he pulled the seat of government away from the place he had always opposed as his nation's capital. Government employees and their families left first. The merchants dependant upon their business soon followed. By 1843 perhaps two or three hundred people, almost all of them men, remained in the city. Such was the degree of inactivity that one day a herd of buffalo wandered nonchalantly through town.[1] A visitor bemoaned the vacant state of the capitol building by noting the many bats fluttering about within its empty chambers.[2]

Austin's diehards held but one trump card in their struggle to sustain the city: possession of the nation's Land Office records. Although President Houston decried them as traitors, residents refused to part with what they saw as their lifeline to survival. In 1842 Houston tried and failed twice to bring the archives out of Austin. The second attempt resulted in an armed standoff between the President's agents and area residents. A seemingly insignificant incident during that affair months later sparked a deadly conflict.

On December 30, 1842, Eli Chandler, Thomas Smith, and about 20 armed men, operating amidst the confusion of a false Indian alarm, succeeded in spiriting the national archives away from the Land Office on Congress Avenue. The few bystanders witnessing the act were powerless to prevent it, but they did hasten Smith and Chandler on their way with a cannon blast. As frenzied town residents scrambled to organize pursuit, many attempted to commandeer the horse of any rider passing by. When one Dr. Marsden refused to yield his animal, "Irish bully" John Nolan threatened to shoot him. A woman screamed as Nolan lowered his rifle, but Captain Mark Lewis knocked the weapon aside and Marsden fled the scene.[3]

In the weeks that followed, one northern visitor saw Austin devolving into "chaos and crime, if not annihilation . . . men were divided into parties or cliques, then were becoming subdivided, the general tendency was to that state in which each man is the enemy of all others, and all are the enemies of each; a condition of things of which it may be said . . . it constitutes hell." Against this backdrop of ill will, John Nolan evinced a "rancorous hostility" toward Mark Lewis. And, as the northerner noted, "when the whole mind is on fire with malignity, an unexplained word or look is sufficient for murder."[4]

An election for militia officers in July 1843 sparked a showdown between the two antagonists. As dozens of men gathered in front of a boarding house on the south side of Pecan (6th) Street east of Congress Avenue, Lewis and Nolan began a fierce argument. Both men pulled single-shot pistols, fired, and missed. Nolan yanked a knife from his belt but the blade separated from the handle. Lewis had another pistol; this time his aim was true, and Nolan fell dead in the street.[5]

Mark Lewis commanded admiration and respect from most Austin residents. He undoubtedly knew that a jury was unlikely to convict him of murder when so many had witnessed Nolan fire a pistol at him. Lewis therefore gave up his weapons and immediately surrendered himself to the sheriff.

The less popular Nolan nevertheless had supporters of his own. One was a relative, nephew George Barrett. Another was, according to contemporary Noah Smithwick, "a certain lawyer whose inordinate vanity and ambition could ill brook the favors lavished on one whom he chose to consider his rival."[6] This man was Louis P. Cooke.

That a man like Louis Cooke would become involved in a street brawl highlights the rough nature of 19th century frontier Texas. A member of the Third Texas Congress, Cooke served on the five-man commission that selected Waterloo in 1839 as the new seat of government. As Secretary of the Navy, he sat on President Mirabeau Lamar's cabinet. With Sam Houston back in power, Lamar adherent Cooke sought and won a seat as the Travis County representative in the Sixth Congress. For unknown reasons, his experiences in Austin had fostered in him a severe grudge against Mark Lewis.

Noah Smithwick claimed that Louis Cooke had actually manipulated John Nolan into provoking his fatal encounter with Mark Lewis. Whether or not this is true, Cooke teamed up with George Barrett to exact revenge for Nolan's death. The morning after the gunfight on Pecan Street the sheriff led Lewis out of the jail to escort him to a preliminary hearing. At a street crossing, Barrett and Cooke stepped out from behind a building to bar the way. Cooke shouted to the sheriff, "Stand out of the way." Lewis saw the pistols in the hands of his adversaries and asked for an opportunity to defend himself, which Cooke answered with another cry to the sheriff to move aside. When Lewis appealed to the sheriff for protection, the man only shoved Lewis farther into the street. Seeing no other chance of survival, Lewis turned to run. He fell with a bullet from Cooke's gun in his back. To make matters worse, bystander Aleck Peyton[7] was also fatally shot as he tried to intervene on Lewis' behalf.

Barrett and Cooke were both arrested and sent to Bastrop to reduce the risk of a lynching. According to one account, Cooke's trial reached the point of jury deliberation when an armed group of his supporters grew rowdy in the courtroom and threatened violence, causing the judge to flee.[8] Another source states that the jury deadlocked 11-1 against Cooke and a new trial was scheduled.[9]

In December 1843 Louis Cooke escaped his Bastrop prison by taking advantage of a log loosened in the jailhouse wall by one of the guards. The following year he lost an eye during an Indian raid on Corpus Christi. He died of cholera in Brownsville in 1849.

George Barrett also escaped justice. Before his trial for complicity in the murders of Mark Lewis and Aleck Peyton he sawed off his leg irons and fled his Bastrop prison. What happened to him after that is unknown.

The sheriff who had failed to protect Lewis had been well-liked before the incident, but he "found the atmosphere so uncongenial thereafter that he sought fresh fields . . . ."[10] His vigorous denials of having colluded with Cooke and Barrett fell on deaf ears. Whether he was innocent or not, the incident destroyed his reputation and his career in Austin.

VISIT THE SITE

- Mark Lewis killed John Nolan on East 6th (Pecan) Street between Brazos Street and Congress Avenue. ❶❺

- The precise location of Mark Lewis' murder is unknown. He was killed at an intersection while being led from jail to court, but I have been unable to find a reference to the specific site of either building.

ENDNOTES

1. *Telegraph and Texas Register*, May 8, 1844.

2. W. Eugene Hollon, and Ruth Lapham Butler, eds., *William Bollaert's Texas* (Norman: University of Oklahoma Press, 1956), pp. 141-142, 183.

3. *Cincinnati Gazette,* November 2, 1844, City of Austin Collection, Texas State Archives.

4. *Ibid.*

5. Details of this incident are from Noah Smithwick, *The Evolution of a State or Recollections of Old Texas Days* (Austin, University of Texas Press, 1983), pp. 206-207, *Cincinnati Gazette,* November 2, 1844, and Frank Brown, *Annals of Travis County and the City of Austin,* chap. 10, Austin History Center, Austin, Texas.

6. Smithwick, p. 206.

7. Peyton was the son of Angelina Eberly.

8. *Cincinnati Gazette,* November 2, 1844.

9. *Handbook of Texas Online,* s.v. "Cooke, Louis P.," http://www.tshaonline.org/handbook/online/articles/CC/fco53.html (accessed November 20, 2008).

10. Smithwick, p. 209.

100 block of East 6th (Pecan) Street, site of John Nolan's death at the hands of Mark Lewis.

22

A BULLY POKER PLAYER

IN THE SUMMER OF 1843 THE CITY of Austin hovered perilously close to extinction. President Sam Houston's removal of the government in response to two separate Mexican army incursions the previous year had seriously depleted the population. Those whose finances depended upon the departed customers had no choice but to leave as well. Only a determined citizenry's successful thwarting of Houston's attempt to pry national land records from its grasp had preserved Austin's tenuous claim as the official government seat, but the laughable nature of this claim lay exposed in the description by one visitor of the capitol building as "the abode of bats, lizards, and stray cattle."[1] A northern newspaperman, employing typical 19th century hyperbole, breathlessly informed his readers that, "The city of Austin is entirely deserted . . . there is not a single human being residing within it—not one!"[2]

With the city so depopulated, Austin residents' fear of Indian attack escalated. Thus, when someone began beating the alarm drum late one afternoon, men, women, and children hastened to the comparative safety of Bullock's Fort. [3] There they heard that a party of painted Comanche between 100 and 500 strong had occupied a live oak grove on a hill north of the city. [4] Within the walls of Bullock's were only 22 men and boys deemed capable of wielding a weapon. Of the women, six insisted on being armed, as did one ill man. The possession of an 18-pound howitzer bolstered their confidence.

The citizens quickly elected as their leader a certain Captain Coleman, [5] "a small, wiry man of unquestioned bravery and recognized as the best poker player in the country." [6] At sundown, when a lookout spotted four mounted Indians with a white flag approaching along Congress Avenue, Coleman and three other men left the fort to talk to them. The two groups met somewhere between Hickory (8th) and Ash (9th) streets. One of the Indians stepped forward as interpreter and explained that he and his comrades had chased a herd of buffalo to the area before deciding to visit the town and trade for sugar and sweet potatoes. Coleman later claimed to recognize the speaker as a white man who had left Austin two years earlier after stealing some horses. He withheld this recognition, however, and informed the man to return to his party with an invitation to a meeting at Bullock's between leaders of the two sides. Shortly thereafter six armed Comanche appeared at the building's entrance.

As the Indians entered the hall, dim candlelight flickering against the 12-foot ceiling, they would have immediately noticed the howitzer and its attendant, one of the townsfolk dressed in military garb bearing an army musket. Coleman and the man carried out the charade of exchanging sign and countersign before the sentry waved everyone into the next room. A long bench lined either side of this room, like the hallway lit only by candlelight. On one bench sat five Anglos, two of whom wore military uniforms. The Indians took places on the other bench.

Coleman opened the conversation by indentifying the two uniformed men as the commanders of a local military garrison, which of course did not exist. He next asked the purpose of the Indians' visit, pointing out their painted faces and the fact that they traveled without their families. The Indian spokesman repeated the tale of the buffalo hunt, adding that the men's families had fallen behind during the chase and would catch up later. As Coleman pretended to confer with the faux officers an Anglo voice thundered from an adjacent room, "I tell you, men, we would be fools to let a single damned Indian get away. With the soldiers we have and the two companies of rangers, whom we will have in less than two hours, we can surround the hill and, when daylight comes, wipe them from the face of the earth." Another voice quickly hushed the first, but added in a loud whisper, "You might as well go in the other room and tell the red devils what a trap they are in."

Returning to the conversation, Coleman sternly reproached the Indians for stealing horses and murdering a man on Brushy Creek two years earlier after just such a truce as they now discussed. The Indians blamed the incident on another band, but this did not appease Coleman. He stood and approached the other side of the room, telling the Comanche that he had no desire to trade with them and that, "You have come here today with a lie in your heart to commit murder and robbery and we are prepared to meet you on your own terms." Sensing the meaning of Coleman's tirade even before hearing the translation, the Indians also rose. Coleman ordered the group from the building. As the Indians crowded toward the doorway, Coleman confronted the interpreter, "John Loflin, you white-livered renegade, I want to tell you that I shall make it my especial duty tomorrow to tack your scalp to a live oak tree on capitol hill."

By sunrise the next morning the Comanche had quit the area. Their true intentions can never be ascertained, but Austin residents at the time believed only that they would have been attacked save for the bold actions of Captain Coleman. As one grateful man reportedly exclaimed while thumping Coleman on the shoulder, "Captain, I knowed you was a bully poker player, but damned if I thought you could bluff a royal flush with a pair of deuces."[7]

VISIT THE SITES

- Richard and Mary Bullock's hotel occupied the northwest corner of Congress Avenue and Pecan (6th) Street. ❾

- Captain Coleman held his first parley with the Comanche while standing in the middle of Congress Avenue between Hickory (8th) and Ash (9th) streets. ⓮

- The Comanche camped atop the hill upon which the present capitol sits. In those days a large grove of live oak trees grew at the summit. ❸

ENDNOTES

1. W. Eugene Hollon, and Ruth Lapham Butler, eds., *William Bollaert's Texas* (Norman: University of Oklahoma Press), p. 198.

2. *Cincinnati Gazette,* November 2, 1844.

3. The hotel built in 1839 by Richard and Mary Bullock on the northwest corner of Congress Avenue and Pecan (6th) Street was one of the largest buildings in town. For more on the Bullocks and their hotel, see the chapter "Bullock's Fort."

4. Details of this incident are from William Walsh, who put his recollections of early Austin life to paper in 1924. Walsh moved to Austin with his family at the age of four in 1840. Numerical counts of Indians in 19th century writing vary widely and often seem greatly exaggerated. One suspects that this is the case here. *The Austin Statesman,* March 16, 1924.

5. Coleman at the time was recovering from wounds inflicted in an earlier Indian fight.

6. *The Austin Statesman,* March 16, 1924.

7. *Ibid.*

Captain Coleman parlayed with Comanche leaders here on Congress Avenue between 8th (Hickory) and 9th (Ash) streets.

23

CAPTAIN COLEMAN'S LUCKY BREAK

ONE DAY IN 1843,[1] **AUSTIN RESIDENT** Mrs. W. M. Thompson decided to pay a visit to James Smith and his family. Because the two-mile ride to Smith's farm led through open country, Mrs. Thompson sought the protection of William Bell and Captain Coleman. The two men dropped Thompson off in the morning with the promise of returning later that day.

Toward sundown, Bell and Coleman hitched up a carriage and began their ride to Smith's place by proceeding east on Pine (5th) Street. At about that same time, a Mrs. Whipple, standing atop President Hill,[2] spied a large group of mounted Indians a mile or so to the east. Mistaking the group for a party of whites, she raised no alarm. A short distance beyond Waller Creek Bell and Coleman entered a stretch of ground known as "the sand hills."[3] Slowed by the sandy nature of the soil, the pair must have seemed easy prey to their Indian attackers. When the carriage was about 400 yards east of the creek the Indians charged. Leaping quickly from the vehicle, Bell and Coleman frantically raced into a nearby corn field. Pursuers quickly caught and killed Bell. Coleman was able to surrender and avoid an immediate death but surely had little hope of long term survival. His captors stripped his clothes and, prodding the naked man with spears, urged him toward an unknown fate.

Penira Brown and her 14-year-old daughter Philian witnessed the attack from the doorway of the DeMorse house on East Avenue.[4] Terrified, the two ladies hid themselves in the brush along the creek, where they remained for several hours. Nolan Luckett's son and a young slave boy were less fortunate. As their comrades were taking care of Bell and Coleman, a number of the attacking Indians saw the boys driving some cows in the distance, sped past the cornfield, and chased them toward the Luckett house. Caught in the open on foot, the boys had little chance of escape. One Indian captured the slave; another sent an arrow into the back of the Luckett boy, who died a few days later.

Joseph Hornsby and James Edmonson had ridden horses out of Austin along East Pine Street sometime after Bell and Coleman. Unseen by the Indians, they witnessed the attack from their position on the road closer to town. One of the young men was unarmed while the other had only a single pistol.[5] With no time to fetch help because the sun was setting, Hornsby and Edmonson knew that if they were to rescue Coleman they would have to do so alone. One of them brandished the pistol; both yelled wildly as they recklessly charged straight at the superior force of Indians. Confused by the sudden racket, the Indians dispersed, allowing Coleman to safely flee. Aroused by the shouting and pistol shot, Austin residents organized a chase party. The Indians raced north for about two miles before crossing Waller Creek and heading west. Hornsby and Edmonson stayed on their tail, screaming continuously in an effort to attract assistance. The posse intercepted the Indians in the vicinity of present day Hyde Park. In the ensuing fight Joseph Hornsby's horse was killed while three Indian mounts were captured. Darkness ended the battle, and the remaining Indians escaped through the western hills.

VISIT THE SITE

- Indians attacked Coleman and Bell on present day East 5th (Pine) Street between Brushy and San Marcos streets. ㉒

- The site of the DeMorse house is now covered by Interstate Highway 35. It probably sat between 2nd (Live Oak) and 3rd (Cypress) streets. Mrs. Brown and her daughter found refuge in Waller Creek directly to the west of the house. ㉓

- J. W. Wilbarger claims that the posse intercepted the party of Indians "about where the fair grounds are now situated."[6] Monroe Shipe purchased the state fairgrounds in the late 19th century and eventually used the land to create the Hyde Park development. The original neighborhood was bounded by Guadalupe, 38th and 45th streets and Avenue H. ⑭

ENDNOTES

1. J. W. Wilbarger provides a date of January 1, 1843. Frank Brown recalls that the incident occurred June 2, 1843. J. W. Wilbarger, *Indian Depredations in Texas* (Austin: Eakin Press, 1985), p. 142, and Frank Brown, *Annals of Travis County and the City of Austin, chap. 10,* Austin History Center, Austin, Texas Austin.

2. President Hill held the presidential mansion built in 1839 for Mirabeau Lamar. Town planner Edwin Waller chose the spot because of its position overlooking the city and the river below. The square block is bounded by Brazos, San Jacinto, Bois d'Arc (7th) and Hickory (8th) streets.

3. Brown, chap. 10.

4. Frank Brown states that this house was owned by the DeMorse family and that it was close to Waller Creek. He adds that Mrs. Brown and her daughter were about 200 yards from the spot of the attack. In those days Waller Creek made an eastward bend at Cypress (3rd) Street, ran south for about a block and curved sharply back westward at Live Oak (2nd) Street, making this block the most likely location of the house. *Ibid.*

5. Pistols at that time were single shot.

6. Wilbarger, p. 144.

Looking west along East 5th (Pine) Street from San Marcos Street. Indians attacked Bell and Coleman at this location as they returned to Austin.

Penira and Philian Brown hid from Indians in this section of Waller Creek between 2nd (Live Oak) and 3rd (Cypress) streets. The DeMorse house from which they fled sat along East Avenue, since replaced by Interstate 35 in the distance.

William Bell's grave in Oakwood Cemetery at 1601 Navasota Street.

24

A YOUNG GIRL'S DEATH

AUSTIN'S EARLIEST RESIDENTS understood that their city lay in unconquered Comanche territory. Writing years after the fact, Julia Lee Sinks recalled her feeling of dread as she neared Austin for the first time

> We approached the city in the late afternoon with relieved fears, for the road traveled for many miles being within the Indian range and so frequently crossed by moccasin tracks, our poetical fancy of the 'noble Indian' had given way to a sickening fear and now with a quick transition of feeling from fear to safety, we were almost jubilant with the thought that we had at last reached a haven of rest in a smiling, peaceful valley . . . .[1]

Before meeting and marrying George Sinks, Julia Lee settled with her family in a cabin on West Pecan (6th) Street. There she would have come to know her immediate neighbor Mrs. Simpson, a widow living with two sons and a daughter on West Pecan three blocks west of Congress Avenue.

Mrs. Simpson kept a few milk cows at her home. Grazing the animals offered her no difficulty, as there was plenty of grass between her house and Shoal Creek to the west. In fact, beyond the Simpson and Lee homes lay little but undeveloped countryside. Standing in her yard peering westward, Mrs. Simpson would have seen only miles of greenery leading to Mount Bonnell, which blocked the view beyond. She would undoubtedly have shuddered at the occasional sight of one or more Indians galloping on horseback in the distance.[2]

November 10, 1844, found the eldest Simpson boy away at Fayette County working for an uncle.[3] Around 3 in the afternoon[4] Mrs. Simpson instructed her other two children, 12-year-old Tommie and 14-year-old Emma, to bring the cows in from Shoal Creek for milking. After finding their quarry near a small branch of the creek the pair began driving them back toward the house. Whether Mrs. Simpson actually saw what happened next or merely responded to her children's shouts is unclear, but what is certain is that several Indians suddenly sprang from the bushes, snatched the children, mounted horses, and sped away toward Mount Bonnell.

Mrs. Simpson's cries of anguish stirred immediate action. Several men[5] organized a rescue party and gave mounted pursuit; others boldly but foolishly started out on foot. Bits of Emma's clothing marked the trail, triggering heartache in her would-be rescuers. The kidnappers raced to the northwest, passing near what is now the intersection of Niles Road and Woodlawn Street, site of the Pease mansion, before reaching Mount Bonnell. Here the pursuit party came close enough to see the mounted Indians scrambling up the hillside in the lead. Once they disappeared over the ridge, however, the Indians had escaped, for the rocky terrain atop Mount Bonnell disguised all traces of their passage. Unable to pick up the trail, the dejected pursuers reluctantly gave up and returned to Austin empty-handed.

Within a few miles of hard riding the kidnappers must have realized they had eluded their pursuers, for they paused at the watering hole later known as Spicewood Springs. By then Tommie had realized the futility of further resistance; his sister, however, had not. While his captors sipped water from the springs, Tommie attempted unsuccessfully to calm his terrified sibling. At last one of the Indians had had enough. He forced the girl onto a horse, which he also mounted and rode up a nearby hill. When the man returned minutes later, the bloody scalp hanging from his saddle told Tommie that he would face captivity alone.

Tommie Simpson remained a captive for 18 months, at which point he was returned to his mother by other Indians that had traded for the boy in Taos. After telling the story of his kidnapping to horrified Austin residents, he led them back to the scene of his sister's murder. There, on a small rise near the intersection of modern Spicewood Springs Road and MoPac Expressway, Judge Joseph Lee recovered the remains of the Simpson girl, minus the scalp last seen hanging from the saddle of her killer.

Later telling of this tale by contemporary John S. "Rip" Ford paints a vivid picture of Anglo-Texan attitudes toward the region's native inhabitants. Reflecting upon the pursuit party's unpleasant task of informing Mrs. Simpson of their failure, Ford lamented that Tommie and Emma would "be subject to all the brutal cruelties and outrages of a captivity a thousand times more terrible than the pangs of death." Emma's death aroused in him fears of her being raped by men he scorned as "barbarians." "No one will ever know the details of the bloody deed," he observed. "Indeed, a knowledge of Indian customs justifies the belief that the sacrifice of an innocent life involved incidents of a more revolting character than mere murder." But "thankfully," Ford concluded, brave pioneers like the Simpsons "reclaimed Texas from the dominion of the Indian and made it the abode of civilized men."[6]

VISIT THE SITES

- According to Frank Brown, the Simpson family lived in a house on West Pecan Street "at the corner many years later occupied by Dr. Swearingen as a residence."[7] Interestingly, this is also the location he gave as the residence of Alphonse de Saligny during the Pig War of 1841. The site in question is the southeast corner lot at the intersection of Guadalupe and West 6th (Pecan) streets. **⓭**

- The creek branch at which the Simpson children found the family cows is now underground, cutting north to south through the block bounded by Nueces, San Antonio, West 7th (Bois d'Arc), and West 8th (Hickory) streets. **⓮**

- Indians captured the children one block to the east, on the southern slope of what is now the historic Bremond block. **㉑**

- Spicewood Springs, now dry, lies in a creek bed immediately south of Spicewood Springs Road and west of North MoPac Expressway. The high ground above the creek upon which the Simpson girl was killed is covered by an office building and parking lot. Wood Hollow Drive or Executive Center Boulevard provides access to the lot. There is no marker. **⑬**

ENDNOTES

1. Julia Lee Sinks vertical file, Barker Center for American History, The University of Texas at Austin.

2. *Ibid.* Julia Lee Sinks writes, "Our home was on the beaten track of the Indians into town from the pass of Mount Bonnell. The knolls beyond the quarry branch were interspersed with timber, and sometimes though not often, we would see galloping past the open spaces beyond the blanketed Indian. The path along the quarry branch, secluded as it was, became their main inlet to the town. It was a sheltered road, never traveled at night by whites, so the Indians claimed right of way, and all full moons brought moccasin tracks in abundance."

3. J. W. Wilbarger, *Indian Depredations in Texas* (Austin: Eakin Press, 1985, reprint of the original published in 1889), pp. 139-140. Wilbarger's account of this incident is the most detailed I have come across. He erroneously writes that the kidnapping occurred in 1842. The November 14, 1844, issue of *The Morning Star* contains a report stating that the episode took place "on Sunday last."

4. W. C. Walsh, *Austin in the Making,* eighth installment, *The Austin Statesman,* March 16, 1924.

5. Among the pursuers were Judge Joseph Lee, Columbus Browning, and Thomas Wooldridge. John Henry Brown, *Indian Wars and Pioneers of Texas* (Austin: L. E. Daniell, 1880), p. 102.

6. *Ibid.,* pp. 101-102.

7. Frank Brown, *Annals of Travis County and the City of Austin,* chap. 10, Austin History Center, Austin, Texas.

Southeast corner of Guadalupe and West 6th (Pecan) streets, site of the Simpson home in 1844.

Indians captured the Simpson children here on West 7th (Bois d'Arc) Street between Guadalupe and San Antonio streets.

Indians killed 14-year-old Emma Simpson here at Spicewood Springs near the modern intersection of MoPac Expressway and Spicewood Springs Road.

A NOTE ON STREET NAMES

WITH INPUT FROM MIRABEAU LAMAR, Edwin Waller, the man appointed by President Lamar to manage Austin's construction, named the city's streets at its 1839 founding. With a few exceptions, Waller chose Texas trees to label the east-west streets and Texas rivers for those oriented north to south in the square grid. The north-south exceptions included the boundary streets West Avenue and East Avenue, as well as the town's major artery Congress Avenue. Waller called the east-west road adjacent to the Colorado River Water Street, the northern boundary North Avenue, and the street on which land had been set aside for a school College Avenue. In 1887 the city changed the names of the east-west streets by numbering them, beginning with 1st Street at the river. First Street was renamed Cesar Chavez Street in 1993. The construction of Interstate Highway 35 obliterated East Avenue.

1839	2010
Water Street	Cesar Chavez Street*
Live Oak Street	2nd Street
Cypress Street	3rd Street
Cedar Street	4th Street

*This was called 1st Street between 1887 and 1993.

Pine Street	5th Street
Pecan Street	6th Street
Bois d'Arc Street	7th Street
Hickory Street	8th Street
Ash Street	9th Street
Mulberry Street	10th Street
Mesquite Street	11th Street
College Avenue	12th Street
Peach Street	13th Street
Walnut Street	14th Street
North Avenue	15th Street
East Avenue	Interstate Highway 35

INDEX
(Italicized page numbers indicate references in photo captions.)

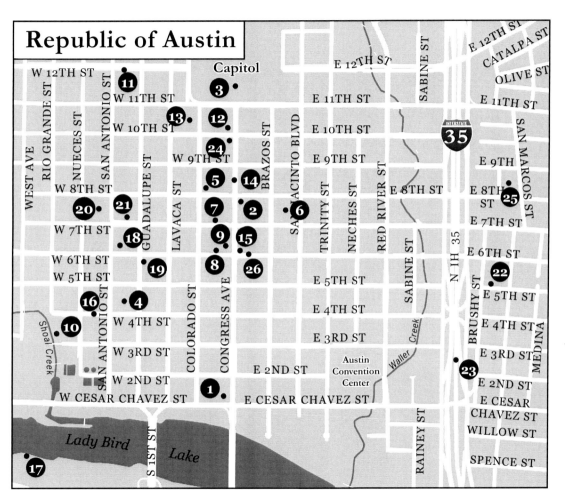

Numbers on the map correspond to those in the "Visit the Sites" section at the end of each chapter.

Order more copies of THE REPUBLIC OF AUSTIN

There are a number of ways to do this:

1. Fill out the form below, and mail with payment to:

   AHCA/Waterloo Press
   P.O. Box 2287
   Austin TX 78768

2. Visit the Waterloo Press online store at http://www.ahca.net and purchase the books via paypal.

3. Call the AHCA/Waterloo Press office at (512) 974-7499 and order with credit card directly over the phone.

4. Call also for purchase of large numbers for 10% discount.

ORDER FORM

Name _____

Phone Number _____   Email Address _____

Number of Copies _____ @ $20.00 per copy   = $ _____

Tax (8.25%) for $20 = $1.65

Purchasing 1 copy = Tax of $ 1.65   Purchasing 2 copies = Tax of $3.30
Purchasing 3 copies = Tax of 4.95   Purchasing 4 copies = Tax of 6.60
Purchasing 5 copies = Tax of 7.25   = $ _____

Add $5.00 for shipping and handling (for 5 books or fewer)   = $ _5.00_
(call (512) 974-7499 for s/h fees for larger orders)

                                        TOTAL   = $ _____

Please include check payment
(Please do not send cash in the mail.)

If using credit card:

Account Number _____   Expiration Date _____

Signature _____

All credit card information is destroyed immediately after transaction.
Please allow seven days for arrival.

WATERLOO PRESS